Developing a Foundation for Learning with Internationally Adopted Children

This practice-focused guide introduces *The SmartStart Toolbox* as a remedial program to help mental health professionals and adoptive parents promote the educational and social development of internationally adopted children aged 4–8.

Recognizing the cultural, emotional, and cognitive needs of children who have experienced a fundamental change in their social situation of development following international adoption, *The SmartStart Toolbox* provides a range of family-based remedial activities which stimulate children's thinking and learning while creating scaffolded attachment opportunities during early interactions with their adoptive families. The volume details the notions of "psychological tools" (Vygotsky) and "mediated learning experience" (Feuerstein) which form the theoretical foundations for *The SmartStart Toolbox* and offers step-by-step guidance on conducting activities and adapting them to the individual child. The *SmartStart* methodology can also be used by professionals for diagnostic purposes.

This text will benefit researchers in child psychology, as well as clinicians, family therapists, social workers, and educators with an interest in child development, cognitive and language enhancement, and adoption and fostering more broadly. Adoptive parents will also benefit from this book and its focus on themes of attachment, parenting, and the development of social cognition.

Boris Gindis is a licensed psychologist, specializing in Childhood Trauma and Psychology of International Adoption.

Carol S. Lidz is a retired licensed psychologist and nationally certified school psychologist, consultant/trainer in Dynamic Assessment.

Routledge Research in Psychology

This series offers an international forum for original and innovative research being conducted across the field of psychology. Titles in the series are empirically or theoretically informed and explore a range of dynamic and timely issues and emerging topics. The series is aimed at upper-level and post-graduate students, researchers, and research students, as well as academics and scholars.

Recent titles in the series include:

Eastern European Perspectives on Emotional Intelligence
Current Developments and Research
Edited by Lada Kaliská and John Pellitteri

The Psychological Basis of Moral Judgments
Philosophical and Empirical Approaches to Moral Relativism
John J. Park

Developing a Model of Islamic Psychology and Psychotherapy
Islamic Theology and Contemporary Understandings of Psychology
Abdallah Rothman

Human Interaction with the Divine, the Sacred, and the Deceased
Psychological, Scientific, and Theological Perspectives
Edited by Thomas G. Plante and Gary E. Schwartz

Developing a Foundation for Learning with Internationally Adopted Children
Family-Based Activities for Remedial Learning and Attachment
Boris Gindis and Carol S. Lidz

For a complete list of titles in this series, please visit: www.routledge.com/Routledge-Research-in-Psychology/book-series/RRIP

Developing a Foundation for Learning with Internationally Adopted Children

Family-Based Activities for Remedial Learning and Attachment

Boris Gindis and Carol S. Lidz

Routledge
Taylor & Francis Group

NEW YORK AND LONDON

First published 2022
by Routledge
605 Third Avenue, New York, NY 10158

and by Routledge
2 Park Square, Milton Park, Abingdon, Oxon OX14 4RN

Routledge is an imprint of the Taylor & Francis Group, an informa business

Library of Congress Cataloging-in-Publication Data
A catalog record for this title has been requested

ISBN: 9781032182476 (hbk)
ISBN: 9781032182513 (pbk)
ISBN: 9781003253587 (ebk)

DOI: 10.4324/9781003253587

Typeset in Times New Roman
by Newgen Publishing UK

It is nice to have a tool!
© C. S. Lidz

The food is on the table.
I'll eat it when I'm able.
It is nice to have a tool!

I need to fix my car.
It won't go very far.
It is nice to have a tool!

My painting's on the wall.
I don't want it to fall.
It is nice to have a tool!

I love to spend the hours
In my garden planting flowers.
It is nice to have a tool!

My child seems very smart
But needs a good strong start.
It is nice to have a tool!

Contents

About the Authors   viii

Introduction: The SmartStart Toolbox Program   1

1   What We Have Learned from Three Decades of
    International Adoption on a Large Scale   4

2   Theoretical Background and Specific Features of
    The SmartStart Toolbox Program   14

3   Seven Units of The SmartStart Toolbox Program   23

4   The SmartStart Toolbox Program as a Basis for
    Diagnosis and Prescription   97

    Conclusion: How the SmartStart Toolbox Differs
    from Other Remedial Programs   111

Index   113

About the Authors

Boris Gindis received his doctorate in Developmental Psychology at the Moscow Academic Research Institute of Psychology and has completed postdoctoral training in School Psychology at the City University of New York. Dr. Gindis is a licensed psychologist in the states of NY and AZ, and is a nationally certified bilingual (Russian/English) school psychologist. Dr. Gindis is specializing in clinical work and research in the field of Complex Childhood Trauma and International Adoption. He was a full professor (currently retired) and director of Bilingual Program at Touro College, NY. Dr. Gindis was the founder and Chief Psychologist at the Center for Cognitive-Developmental Assessment and Remediation (2021), located in NY and AZ. He is the author of a book *Child Development Mediated by Trauma: The Dark Side of International Adoption*, Routledge, 2019, NY. Dr. Gindis is the author of published articles and book chapters, including a comprehensive volume *Vygotsky's Theory of Education in Cultural Contexts,* Cambridge University Press, 2003 (with coauthors and coeditors). Dr. Gindis has served as a guest-editor for psychology journals and has been a keynote speaker at national and international conferences. He currently lives in Sedona, AZ, and continues with clinical practice, research, and publications in the field of Child Psychology. To learn more about Dr. Gindis and his clinical services and research please visit www.bgcenter.com.

Carol S. Lidz is currently retired after a 40-year career as a school psychologist in a wide variety of settings. She obtained her BA in Psychology from the University of Michigan, her MA in School Psychology from the University of Tennessee, and her Psy.D. in School Psychology from Rutgers University's Graduate School of Applied Professional Psychology. Beginning as a frontline psychologist in Monmouth County (NJ) school districts, she worked as a school psychologist for the Montgomery County (PA) Intermediate Unit and a pediatric psychologist for Moss Rehabilitation Hospital. She then was invited to design and direct the Head Start Clinic Team, administered by United Cerebral Palsy Association of Philadelphia and Vicinity, followed by joining the School Psychology faculty at Temple University to lead their new specialization in Early Childhood. Finally, she joined the team formed by Touro College to create and direct their School Psychology Program within the new Graduate School of Psychology and Education, where she became a full professor. She has authored seven books, mostly on topics related to early childhood and dynamic assessment, and has published a number of articles and research studies primarily related to her two procedures: the Application of Cognitive Functions Scale and the Mediated Learning Experience Rating Scale. Her primary areas of research have been dynamic assessment and parent–child interaction.

Figure 0.01 Dr. Carol Lidz and Dr. Boris Gindis work on the SmartStart project.

Introduction
The SmartStart Toolbox Program

The book *Developing a Foundation for Learning with Internationally Adopted Children/Family-Based Activities for Remedial Learning and Attachment* is written for two distinct categories of users: professionals (adoption agency workers, child psychologists, social workers, psychotherapists, family therapists/counselors, educators/remedial specialists working with international adoptees either directly or through adoptive families) and parents of internationally adopted post-institutionalized children who are a very special group – highly educated and greatly motivated – caregivers. The goal of this Program is to help adoptive parents and professionals implement family-based activities that form the basis for educational and social remediation of children adopted from orphanages outside of the United States.

The full name of this methodology is *The SmartStart Toolbox Program*. It is based on the cognitive education curriculum for preschoolers called "Let's Think About It!" originally developed by Dr. Carol S. Lidz and Lisa Chase-Childers in 1998 in collaboration with St. Luke's School in New York City. The program was then adapted for use with parents of children with hearing impairment by Dr. Lidz, in collaboration with Dr. Janice Berchin-Weiss and the staff of the Lexington School for Hearing Impaired in New York. The current manual has been substantially revised, supplemented, and modified by Dr. Carol S. Lidz and Dr. Boris Gindis to address the needs of professionals working with parents of internationally adopted children of preschool, kindergarten, and early primary ages.

The objectives of The SmartStart Toolbox Program are to build, remediate, and stimulate thinking, learning, and language in internationally adopted children while creating and facilitating the attachment between the adopted children and their adoptive parents. The program, through mediational interactions with their parents, provides

DOI: 10.4324/9781003253587-1

internationally adopted children with the internal tools to further their development of self-regulation, active learning, abstract thinking, competent symbol use, and strategic problem-solving. The program focuses on aspects of adult-child interactions during the activities of each of the units that have been found to influence the cognitive development of young children in a positive way and, at the same time, strengthen their emotional bonds with their parents. To call these objectives cognitive is not to ignore or downplay the importance of emotions that are an important ingredient of effective teaching and learning. Connecting learning to emotion is an essential component of a successful mediation, even more so for children who have experienced deprivation and trauma in the early, most formative, years of their lives.

The book consists of an Introduction, four chapters, and Conclusion.

Chapter 1 discusses the specifics of psycho-educational issues of internationally adopted children ages four through eight and the two basic concepts of *school readiness* and *remediation*, in the context of international adoption.

Chapter 2 presents the theoretical foundation of the methodology behind the activities that comprise The SmartStart Toolbox Program.

Chapter 3 contains the core of the program: seven units of activities aimed at scaffolding learning and attachment in international adoptees. Each unit starts with a brief explanation of the theoretical underpinning that relates to the core of that Unit. This is followed by the goals around which the activities of that Unit are designed. Detailed descriptions of each activity go along with the suggestions for the users (parents and professionals) to inform them of the materials needed and the instructions for guiding the children through the activity. Please note that the directions for these activities are at times a bit wordy for a child who is still struggling with learning English. The directions are mainly for the parents and professionals so that they better manage their role as a mediator for the activity. Users should feel free to demonstrate, reduce, or substitute words as appropriate for the child. They should do whatever they see fit to communicate the nature of the activities to the child. Each unit is accompanied by a vocabulary list of suggested words for mediators to use during the course of the activities. Vocabulary building is considered to be an essential element in the development of cognitive skills, self-regulated behavior, and attachment. Parents are encouraged to integrate this vocabulary into their ongoing communications with their children and to carry these words across the units and into everyday life. Each unit is designed to support and create opportunities for the development of increased attachment between newly adopted children and their adoptive parents through participation in joint/shared activities within a positive emotional context. The specific activities were selected and designed to be extensions of what parents would ordinarily do with their children, using materials that are readily available. The focus of each unit is on the opportunities for a pleasant interaction between parents and their children while engaging in activities that offer opportunities that enhance the child's development and adjustment to their new social/cultural environment.

Chapter 4 describes the use of The SmartStart Toolbox Program as a diagnostic-prescriptive instrument by professionals who are trained within their disciplines, such as psychology, education, social work.

The attentive reader will notice variations in writing styles that occur throughout this book. Although the targeted readership is mental health professionals, we also had in mind adoptive parents as the users of this methodology. This book is designed to present a practical, hands-on program that is easily understood and followed by a diverse audience. We wish to be clear that the program reflects a foundation of current theory and research generated by academic sources. Therefore, the style of writing for the professionals is necessarily more formal and "academic," whereas, the more applied portions of the book are necessarily more casual and friendly to the adoptive parents. The actual activities (Chapter 3) are presented in everyday vivid and lucid language, specifically to be understood by children when used by parents or a therapist leading a group of parents through the activities with their children. The "What do I say; What do I do?" section of every activity is specifically worded to direct the parent to use the keywords when talking to their child. We consider the accessibility of our material and the means of its delivery to be valuable attributes of our program.

The forms within this book can be used or replicated for personal or professional use only.

1 What We Have Learned from Three Decades of International Adoption on a Large Scale

This chapter discusses the specifics of psycho-educational issues of internationally adopted children ages four through eight and the two basic concepts: *school readiness* and *remediation* in the context of international adoption. Repetitive psychological traumatization along with educational deprivation and social/emotional neglect in early childhood mediates an adopted child's development by creating distortions and impairments in all-important school-related capacities to form social relations, to advance cognitively and academically, and to behave within socially accepted norms. Proper understanding of the consequences of profound childhood trauma is a must in the successful rehabilitation and remediation of international adoptees. Within the last decade, international adoption has changed its qualitative and quantitative characteristics: special needs and "older" (adopted after their third birthday) children will constitute the largest percentage of children available for international adoption. One of the challenges faced by parents of internationally adopted preschool and elementary school-age children is their preparation for formal school education. The SmartStart Toolbox Program responds to the question of what children need to master in order to become competent learners within the formal school context.

Over 30 years (1989–2021) of international adoption on a large scale is a long time, and over half a million children adopted in North America (United States and Canada) from the overseas orphanages is a big number. What are the lessons we have learned so far?

First, mere removal of a young child from an environment of neglect and deprivation is not a guarantee of positive outcomes. Repetitive traumatization in the context of human relationships done in early childhood impacts the child's development by creating distortions and impairments that are difficult and at times just impossible to remediate. Internationally adopted children are at high risk for Developmental

DOI: 10.4324/9781003253587-2

Trauma Disorder (Van der Kolk, 2005; Gindis, 2019). This causes distortions in all important abilities to form social relations, advance cognitively/academically, and behave within socially acceptable norms.

Second, the majority of children who spend their early years in foreign orphanages have developed certain behaviors (in fact, "survival skills") that they use to handle their new environment after adoption. These patterns of behavior are often misinterpreted as oppositional defiant behaviors, or mood disorder, or hyperactivity, or even as autistic spectrum, and therefore mistakenly treated with ineffective behavioral management techniques or medication. Proper understanding of the consequences of a profound complex childhood trauma is a must in the successful rehabilitation and remediation of international adoptees.

Third, internationally adopted children from developing countries soon after arrival enter one of the most advanced educational systems in the world. Coping with school issues and competing against the middle-class native speakers of English, constitute still more links in the long chain of traumatization. For the majority of children adopted at or close to school age, regular education programs are often beyond their readiness and should be supplemented or even replaced by remediation. Before these children join a mainstream classroom, they need to be emended to be able to take advantage of a regular curriculum.

Fourth, internationally adopted children have experienced the most severe form of neglect that can influence their development for many years of their post-adoption life. Still, the human mind and body have immense resources and resilience. The effect of a socially induced traumatic environment is influential but not final; in most cases the consequences of adverse childhood experience can be rehabilitated, depending on the degree of damage and the nature of the rehabilitation methods. Working with international adoptees, the parents, educators, and mental health professionals should strive to strengthen the many positive existing aspects of the children's functioning, preserve coping mechanisms that may have served them well in the past while developing new skills and knowledgebase that can promote their ability to deal with their new circumstances. International adoptees need therapeutic parenting in the family, intensive and focused remediation at school, and highly specialized mental health service, if needed, in the community. They challenge us to find better treatments for rehabilitation and remediation, and motivate us to work on expanding the boundaries of restoration for all children afflicted by trauma.

The cumulative experience of the last three decades of international adoption on a large scale in Western countries has provided evidence that international adoption is not simply an event, but a process of restoration of physical health, emotional stability, mental capacity, and learning capability of former orphanage inmates.

Within the last decade, just before the onset of the COVID-19 plague, international adoption changed its qualitative and quantitative characteristics, with one distinct trend that will likely prevail in the foreseeable post-pandemic future: special needs and "older" (adopted after their third birthday) children will likely constitute the largest percentage of children available for international adoption. For this growing segment of international adoptees, the synergetic efforts of the adoptive parents, school personnel, mental health professionals, and state-run supportive agencies are a must for the success of each and every case of international adoption. No less important are the methods of remediation for international adoptees. These include the teaching procedures and parenting techniques that are needed to scaffold the victims of prolonged neglect and deprivation into self-sufficiency and productive learning. The description of one of such methodology, verified through nearly two decades of implementation, is contained in this book.

Remediation in the Context of International Adoption

In this Manual the notion of "remediation" is the most basic concept. To "remediate" means to correct something that is deficient, to make up for a lack of something, to overcome the issues that prevent successful functioning. The goal of remediation is to correct cognitive and academic deficits to the point where these no longer constitute an obstacle to age-appropriate functioning. In practical terms, remediation involves re-teaching the child to use special methodologies that differ from those of mainstream teaching/learning. In the case of international adoptees, remedial methods and services are therapeutic in nature, thus aiming to address the consequences of neglect, trauma, and deprivation typical for the majority of international adoptees.

In creating The SmartStart Toolbox Program we assure that this is not meant to be a "can't do" program for either the children or their parents. Both have considerable skills and abilities already within their repertories. Therefore, we do not recommend that parents focus on what the child can't do, nor to view the suggestions as giving the parent something not already within their skill range. We would like each user, be it a parent or a therapist, to view the suggestions as extensions of what is already within their capabilities, using the ideas as extensions, and viewing the units and the goals as checklists that serve as benchmarks for developmental content that promise to promote the further development of their child. It is therefore not recommended that parents select only those activities that challenge their children. On the contrary, it is recommended that the activities include behaviors and materials that the children can already do, and, if not totally, then can serve as a starting point for further development. Motivation is strongly related to feelings of competence. Learning should therefore begin within the child's (and parent's or a therapist's) current level of functioning, and then gradually and carefully move to the next level. It will not be rewarding for either the user of the program or the child to engage in activities that promise frustration. These should be times of playful and enjoyable shared learning. We also strongly encourage parents and therapists to make their own extensions of the ideas presented here.

"Older" Internationally Adopted Children as the Focus of The SmartStart Toolbox Program

Within the last decade we have observed a decline in the number of children adopted from abroad (U.S. Department of State, Bureau of Consular Affairs report, March 2020). However, the decline in the number of adopted children is limited to children younger than two years (Mounts & Bradley, 2019). The majority of international adoptees within the last 14 years have been children older than 3 years at the time of adoption (U.S. Department of State, Bureau of Consular Affairs report dated March 2020). On their arrival, or soon after arrival, the majority of the new adoptees enter our schools. The education of these students is a real challenge for our educational system.

The emphasis in this Manual is on the so-called "older," "late-adopted," or "school-age" children between the ages of four through eight years who, on arrival, are considered either preschool or early grades students. In other words, these children have already spent at least four years of their early childhood in overseas institutional care, and are to be included in our educational system. These children display certain prominent common features.

Every one of the "older" international adoptees has had to live through painful, trauma-producing experiences in their pre-adoptive life. The authors from the Donaldson Adoption Institute Report accurately observed that:

> Most adopted children, because they suffered early deprivation or maltreatment, come to their new families with elevated risks for developmental, physical, psychological, emotional, or behavioral challenges. Among the factors linked with these higher risks are

the following: prenatal malnutrition and low birth weight, pre-natal exposure to toxic substances, older age at adoption, early deprivation, abuse or neglect, multiple placements, and emotional conflicts related to loss and identity issues.

(Donaldson Adoption Institute, 2010, p. 5)

There needs to be a clear understanding that we are dealing with children whose early childhood has been mediated by complex, prolonged, and severe trauma. This recognition is the basis for their future successful healing and remediation.

Further, the language of the accepting country becomes the adoptees' new native language, while their original language is subjected to rapid attrition. The majority of internationally adopted children start learning their new language several years later than their peers, and their pro-cess of acquisition is different from the "typical" ways of mastering the native language by their peers (Glennen, 2015; Gindis, 2019).

Finally, contrary to popular belief, rather than offering a solution to all of the problems of their pre-adoptive life, the child's arrival in the new motherland introduces new challenges. Radical changes in the social situations of the children's development take place: from insti-tutional care to family life, from extreme deprivation and neglect to an attentive and protective middle-class style of parenting, from native lan-guage and culture to sweeping changes in the cultural/linguistic setting. Family life, with its complex relationships, is uncharted territory for children brought up in orphanages. The American educational system often presents a painful challenge for years to come. Post-adoption trau-matization may also include exposure to a mismatched family, negative school experiences, and rejection by peers.

School Readiness in the Context of International Adoption

One of the challenges faced by parents of internationally adopted pre-school and elementary school-age children is in the preparation of their newly adopted children for formal school education. It is a fact, found and confirmed in numerous research and clinical publications, that internationally adopted children are not ready for their new school experience from many perspectives (for a review see: Gindis, 2019). In addition, these children are so emotionally fragile that they could be fur-ther traumatized when pushed by their adoptive parents' expectations beyond their reach. Their lack of school readiness and emotional fra-gility often predefine academic failure, reinforcing low self-esteem, lack of interest in studying, and constant frustration associated with unsuccessful learning effort.

School readiness is a structured set of competencies relevant to societal expectations of accomplishments for a certain chronological age (Kaufman & Sandilos, 2017). There are no specific selection criteria, universal test, or even commonly agreed-upon set of standards that allow parents and professionals to decide whether a child is ready for formal schooling (Lidz, 1999). Legally, the only requirement for academic placement in the US is the chronological age of the child; thus, children must be five years old by September 1 (or January 1 in some states) for kindergarten entrance, six for first grade, seven for second grade, eight for third grade, and so on. Thus, readiness to some extent depends upon zip code. Readiness is always a range of competencies that may be roughly described as "deficient," "below average," "average," or "above average" in relation to the majority of children of the agreed-upon legal age. This ignores the fact that children learn and develop at different paces, as well as in uneven spurts. As a result, we see children with wide variations in their school-related skills in typical kindergarten through third grades. Although readiness is usually considered mostly in relation to school entry of a young child (five to six years), in the context of international adoption, readiness really needs to be examined for all age levels. In general, for the majority of international adoptees, their readiness for education in our school system could be estimated as "deficient": children who were deprived of enriching experiences during their early years are less able to profit from a learning situation after adoption because of a mismatch between their school readiness and the requirements of the new and advanced learning situation.

Whether or not a child is deemed "ready" typically offers a classification that opens or closes the door to a pre-set program. It rarely relates to what happens to the child who does not pass "go," or, even for that matter, what happens to the children who do. There is little thought about what children need to learn in order to climb the ladder of development of ability to function competently in the society in which they are to function. The SmartStart Toolbox Program does respond to the question of what children need to master in order to become more competent learners within both the formal school context, as well as in greater society. The Program focuses on generalizable processes that underlie the content the children will face in more formal learning situations. For example, the "Nimble Symbol" Unit does not drill the child in the alphabet or numerical figures (these are indeed important, but not for this Program), but instead, focuses on the underlying principle of symbolic representation, for which the letters of the alphabet are only one example.

Basic cognitive skills (such as classification, pattern detection, comparison, association, recognition of similarities and differences, etc.) in typically developing children are formed during their pre-school years with the help of their parents. These cognitive competencies further develop during the school-based learning that follows and form the basis for math, writing, and reading proficiencies. However, in the majority of school-age internationally adopted children, this foundation has not been formed, which makes it much more difficult for them to master literacy skills. These cognitive difficulties are usually associated with certain emotional/behavioral problems. The experiences of cognitive difficulty and constant failure feed upon themselves in a negative spiraling fashion, resulting in low self-esteem, lack of interest, and constant stress associated with frustrated cognitive efforts mentioned above.

The development of social skills and the associated ability to participate in shared activities are important indicators of readiness. The capacity to initiate, respond to, and maintain social interaction is a must in school due to the very nature of the school environment. The typically underdeveloped social skills and overdeveloped emotional vulnerability of international adoptees in the school context makes them less able to tolerate the stresses expected for their age, as they tend to be less capable of self-regulating their goal-directed behavior, and less self-sufficient in overcoming the emotional strain associated with the competitive nature of the school (Julian & McCall, 2016).

International adoptees are particularly below age expectations in their language development. They need not only master the communicative aspects of their new language, but they also must grasp the cognitive/academic aspects needed for profiting from their school education. This is a very difficult task for many international adoptees. A prominent "trademark" of an internationally adopted child in the age group from four through eight is their general weakness in their native (first) language development. It is a well-known fact that the best predictor of new language learning is the level of mastery of the first language (Bialystok, 2001). From this perspective, international adoptees have a "rocky start" from the beginning, unlike their peers among other English language learners, such as children from immigrant families.

Indeed, from the school's perspective, the greatest population "at-risk" for cognitive/academic language problems is the age group between four and eight. Children adopted before the age of three have at least two to three years of development mediated through their new language before entering school. On the other hand, children older than eight years may be literate in their native language and have an opportunity to transfer some of their cognitive language skills into their new language. Also, cognitive language problems in children older than eight are relatively easy to identify, and remediation strategies are likely to be straightforward. Those between four and eight really "fall between the cracks." Their language problems are difficult to pinpoint because they are disguised by the dynamics of second language acquisition that is mostly in the communicative, not the cognitive/academic, area. It should be added that the loss of the first language occurs very fast in this age group, literally within the first three to six months after arrival in a new family. Researchers have found little or no "transfer" of language skills from one language to the other in children of this age group. (Glennen, 2015: Gindis, 2019). This means that, from the beginning, most of the internationally adopted children in this age group need remedial work in the language area.

In addition, children with an institutional background have a huge disadvantage in the development of their academic and pre-academic skills compared to their counterparts living in middle-class families. Orphanage-raised children may not develop certain pre-academic skills (for example, drawing, copying, coloring, and other pencil-and-paper activities) associated with early childhood education, nor develop their related social/behavior self-regulation because they never had an opportunity to learn and practice these skills.

Unfortunately, understanding the need for comprehensive and focused remediation of internationally adopted children is not something shared by all adoptive parents and educational professionals. Some parents believe that all that an adopted child needs are "love and good nutrition." Some adoptive parents hope that, if a child is generally healthy, there should be no problems for him/her in school. Another conviction is that the younger the child at adoption, the less the chance that parents will encounter problems in the child's schooling. Over three decades of research and practical experience with international adoption in the United States show that these assumptions are not true. This leads us to conclude that many, if not all, internationally adopted children in this age group should be screened for possible deficiencies in their readiness for school education.

• However, it is also important to note that we take the position that the absence or underdevelopment of these so-called readiness skills should not be a basis for denial of school entry for the child. Identification of areas of need should suggest areas in need of remediation. Our position on readiness is that children are always ready for learning. There is not always an optimal match between what the school wishes to teach and what the internationally adopted child is prepared to learn. Schools and adoptive families need to work together to identify and develop the school's ability to meet the needs of the children, and the ability of the children to develop the competencies needed for success in school. It is just as important for schools to be ready for children, as it is for children to be ready for school.

It should be standard practice in our schools that, if a former orphan from a foreign country has one of the following "red flags" in her/his orphanage-based records – "delay in psycho-motor development," "delay in language and psychological development," "temporally delayed in psychological development," "specific speech disorders" (for example, poor articulation or stuttering) and other similar descriptions – preschool educational screening and remediation should be "a must" The above notations in pre-adoption documentations are not medical diagnoses per se, but, rather, the terms used to indicate observed deficiencies in the child's development in comparison with peers. The degree of delay may vary from relatively mild to significant (see the review in Gindis, 2019).

It is also necessary to consider the nature and degree of the child's atypical educational history presented in their adoption-related legal and medical documentation. This includes such recorded observations as the child not starting formal schooling on time; or that the child was in a "special" school for neurologically handicapped children, or that the child received remedial services in school; or had been under the "observation" of a specialist (for example, speech pathologist). A definite indicator of special needs is when the child was a resident of a "specialized" orphanage. This is usually related to a corresponding medical diagnosis, but sometimes no specific medical diagnosis is mentioned; however, the very fact that the child was placed in a children's home for "neurologically-impaired" residents is a definite "red flag."

In summary, for children adopted between the ages of four to eight, the expectations are that they will enter kindergarten at the age of five and first grade at the age of six. However, developmentally, many of the international adoptees are delayed in terms of American standards for preschoolers. A post-institutionalized child of a certain chronological age may be much younger developmentally and functionally. Indeed, emotional, cognitive, and behavioral immaturity is the "trademark" of former orphanage residents.

References

Bialystok, E. (2001). *Bilingualism in development: Language, literacy, and cognition.* New York: Cambridge University Press.

Donaldson Adoption Institute (2010). *Keeping the promise: The critical need for post-adoption services to enable children and families to succeed; Policy & Practice Perspective.* Retrieved from: https://affcny.org/wp-content/uploads/EBDKeepingThePromise.pdf.

Gindis, B. (2019). *Child development mediated by trauma: The dark side of international adoption.* New York: Routledge.

Glennen, S. (2015). Internationally adopted children in the early school years: Relative strengths and weaknesses in language abilities. *Language, Speech, and Hearing Services in Schools, 46,* 1–13.

Julian, M. & McCall, R. (2016). Social skills in children adopted from socially-emotionally depriving institutions. *Adoption Quarterly, 19*(1), 44–62.

Kaufman, S. & Sandilos, L. (2017). School transition and school readiness: An outcome of early childhood development. *Encyclopedia of Early Childhood Development.* Retrieved from: www.child-encyclopedia.com/sites/default/files/textes-experts/en/814/school-transition-and-school-readiness-an-outcome-of-early-childhood-development.pdf.

Lidz, C. (1999). School readiness revisited. Rethinking the concept of school readiness: What do children need to know in order to become competent thinkers and metacognitive learners? *NASP Communique, 28,* 24–26.

Mounts, B. & Bradley, L. (2019). Issues involving international adoption. *The Family Journal: Counseling and Therapy for Couples and Families, 29*(1), 33–38.

U.S. Department of State. (March 2020). *Annual report on intercountry adoptions, FY 2019 and previous years.* Washington, DC: Author.

Van der Kolk, B.A. (2005). Developmental trauma disorder: Toward a rational diagnosis for children with complex trauma histories. *Psychiatric Annals, 35*(5), 401–408.

2 Theoretical Background and Specific Features of The SmartStart Toolbox Program

This chapter presents the theoretical foundations of the methodology behind the activities that comprise The SmartStart Toolbox Program. The first paradigm is Vygotsky's ideas on the importance of the social context of learning, the notion of "psychological tools" (hence the title "SmartStart Toolbox"), and the imminence of internalization of culture. The second concept is Feuerstein's "Mediated Learning Experience (MLE)" as specific types of interactions between a mediator (in our context this is an adoptive parent or a therapist) and a child. The mediator, through specific activities presented in The SmartStart Toolbox Program, works within four closely connected directions: enrichment of cognitive language, formation and scaffolding of specific cognitive skills (thus increasing cognitive competence), facilitation of task-intrinsic motivation, and encouragement of self-regulation in goal-directed learning behavior. Mediated interactions between parents and their children provide tools for further development of cognitive and social/emotional domains, while at the same time strengthening the emotional bonds of children with their parents. Connecting learning to emotion is an essential component of successful remediation, even more so for children who have experienced deprivation and trauma in the early, most formative, years of their lives. These two-fold goals are the core of The SmartStart Toolbox Program in remediation and mental health rehabilitation of international adoptees.

The SmartStart Toolbox Program was designed on the basis of what is currently known about best practices in promoting the mental and social development of traumatized and neglected young children. The program emphasizes the importance of the role of the adult in facilitating the development of higher mental functions in children. The ideas are also based on research studies that relate so-called therapeutic parenting practices to the successful preparedness of children for school learning.

DOI: 10.4324/9781003253587-3

One of the stunning findings revealed during the process of working with international adoptees in school was that "typical" remediation (that is, more intense work in a smaller group or individually, using basically the same teaching methodology as in the classroom) is not sufficient and, at times, is even counterproductive (Welsh, Viana, Petrill, & Mathias, 2007; Gindis, 2019). The problem is that conventional remediation "assumes" the existence of an appropriate base in cognition of the students upon whom it tries to build the increasingly complex compensatory structures. However, the very lack of a proper foundation constitutes the major difficulty in the remediation of many internationally adopted children (Rutter, 1999-A)).

A commonly known fact in child psychology is that cognitive abilities tend to be developmentally hierarchical; that is, the advancement of more complex cognitive structures rests upon the prior appearance of more simple cognitive components. Various cognitive skills are expected to have been already developed in children of certain ages. For example, in most families, a typically developing child is involved in pencil-and-paper activities such as coloring, copying, drawing, etc. from the age of two or even earlier. By the age of five, certain grapho-motor skills are expected to have developed. If these skills are underdeveloped, the causes are likely to be found in delays of the child's fine-motor proficiency, visual perception capacity, visual-motor integration, and other abilities, because it is assumed that the child has had age-appropriate opportunities to learn and practice these skills. For internationally adopted children, however, these very opportunities may not be available; therefore, the children have had no chance to learn and practice these skills. Even if the children have developed age-appropriate fine-motor skills and normal visual perceptual abilities, they may still have deficient grapho-motor skills that can negatively impact their writing abilities. The same is true of many of their basic cognitive facilities, such as patterning, classifying, sequencing, etc. The restoration or building from scratch of these basic cognitive capabilities is a prerequisite for a successful remediation.

In general, the remediation of internationally adopted children should be applied from the four closely connected directions reflected in The SmartStart Toolbox Program: enrichment of cognitive language, increasing cognitive competence by mastering specific cognitive skills, facilitation of task-intrinsic motivation, and enhancing self-regulation in goal-directed learning behavior. All of these provide the context for the delivery of an optimal MLE, as described by Feuerstein and his associates (1980).

Immature self-regulation of attention and cognitive effort are typical for many international adoptees in this age group because their independent goal-directed cognitive activity is very limited, and much of their effort is directed to grabbing and retaining an adult's attention and interaction. This is merely a "survival skill" that worked effectively in their former lives as an orphanage inmate where an adult's approval/attention was a highly valued prize. As a result, adopted children in this age group persistently demonstrate "learned helplessness" patterns of behavior by not attempting or refusing to continue to try those cognitive activities that they perceived as difficult for them. The SmartStart methodology is crafted to address these cognitive, motivational, and self-regulation issues. The children can be taught how to inhibit impulsive responses, how to analyze a problem using a certain "algorithm," and how to experiment mentally with the possible solutions of the problem.

In accordance with the "mediational approach" (Haywood & Lidz, 2007), it is not the subject of activity, which is important, but the process of guiding the child in the direction of employing the cognitive effort that is just beyond his/her previous experience. The SmartStart Toolbox Program offers the means for the development of cognitive/academic language, self-regulation (an important indication of emotional, social, and mental maturity), use of symbols (a defining characteristic of the human that pervades literacy, numeracy, and science), reciprocal social interaction (pragmatics of verbal and nonverbal communication, positive social competencies and skills). In terms of specific cognitive skills and operations, the program concentrates on classification, comparison, seriation, and pattern detection, which are all major mental operations in math and science. The student in the program learns the "if … then" connections so substantial in science/math as well in day-to-day social interaction. Finally, the emphasis is on planning/executive functions (ability to engage in goal-directed organized, intentional behavior) and the processes of memory (ability to select and apply the means of deliberate recall of learned material). All these factors are relevant to the formation of the level of competency needed for successful school learning.

The theoretical foundation of The SmartStart Toolbox Program is primarily the ideas of two masterminds of contemporary psychology: Lev Vygotsky and Reuven Feuerstein. From the works of Vygotsky (Vygotsky, 1987–1998; Lidz & Gindis, 2003), we derived the idea of the importance of the social context of learning, the significance of the expert-novice (apprenticeship) interaction, the value of development of language as a tool of thinking, the notion of "psychological tools" (hence the title "SmartStart Toolbox"), and the facilitation of internalization of culture. In the writings of Feuerstein and his associates (1980, 2003), we found delineation of the concept of "MLEs" to describe the specific types of interactions that promote cognitive development. According to both Vygotsky and Feuerstein, adults play a critical role in selecting experiences for children, highlighting what children need to notice about these experiences, presenting these in digestible ways, extracting important principles and messages, and offering support, encouragement, and feedback to promote the development of competence. Deprived of such mediation, children are indeed disadvantaged and "at risk" in their development and ability to move to more advanced levels of learning.

Because MLE (a concept most fully explored by Feuerstein and his associates) has such a pervasive influence on *The SmartStart Toolbox Program*, some further expansion of this concept seems warranted. Basically, MLE describes the kinds of interactions between a more experienced person (parent, teacher, therapist, learning specialist, etc., designated as a "mediator") and a child that promotes the development of higher levels of thinking in the learner. MLE interactions occur when mediators promote awareness of basic principles and strategies of problem-solving and keep in mind that an interaction that involves new learning is more about the child's ability to profit from the experience and less about the perfection of the end product. Indeed, the intent of The SmartStart Toolbox Program is to engage the children in a repertory of MLEs through interactions with their primary mediators (parents, therapists, teachers, etc.). Based on these influences, the SmartStart Toolbox units and their activities were designed to:

- Deliberately expose the child to experiences and ideas that are culturally valued and viewed as important for the development of independent functioning.
- Bring the child's attention to the important features of what should be noticed about these experiences, objects, or ideas.
- Couch/teaching within an emotionally warm, positive, enthusiastic context.
- Communicate clearly about what is to be learned and how best to learn it.
- Promote planning and strategic thinking in the child.
- Provide connections between new ideas and experiences and what the child already knows.
- Bestow connections between the new ideas and experiences and what the child will be doing in the future.
- Offer feedback to the child that is not only positive and encouraging (both of which are important), but that also includes information about what was good (or bad) about what the child did.

- Challenge the child's thinking by posing questions, using vocabulary, communicating ideas that are a bit (not too much) of a stretch for the child, making the child reach just beyond what she or he already knows or can do.
- Responds to the child in a timely and appropriate way.
- Encourages the child's increasing competence and accomplishments that document the child's ability to learn.

Finally, we need to mention two features that make The SmartStart Toolbox the remedial methodology of choice for children who have experienced international adoption.

The first is attachment, the capacity to form and maintain age-appropriate intimate relationships within the family. In international adoption there is no more emotionally charged issue than attachment. Indeed, attachment is the core of adoption, and failed attachment ruins the very nature of adoption. The mainstream understanding is that attachment difficulties are due to pathological care: systematic neglect and deprivation of the child's basic physical and emotional needs for security, comfort, stimulation, and affection in the early, most formative years (DSM 5, 2013).

The vast majority of older internationally adopted children do have the capacity to form an attachment to the newly acquired parents and siblings, but the realization of this capacity requires specific and focused efforts from the adoptive family (Rutter, 1999-B). Initially, adoptive parents and their children meet as strangers, and it would be a miracle if any internationally adopted child were completely attached to the adoptive parents upon arrival or even within the first several months. Attachment is a two-way street that includes attachment of the parents to the child and attachment of the child to his/her adoptive parents. We know that attachment is not a mystical wonder arriving from a thin air, but a complex psychological relationship based on social and emotional interconnectedness between individuals, which is attained through mutual pursuits, interests, and experiences. Based on three decades of working with "older" international adoptees, we have found that shared/joint goal-directed activities of the parents with their children are the most effective ways to form mutual attachment (Gindis, 2019). The units of The SmartStart Toolbox Program suggest specific opportunities for forming the affection, connection, and tenderness (the structured components of attachment) needed for such desired outcomes. Each unit of The SmartStart Toolbox Program is designed to strengthen attachment through engagement in common enjoyable (often playful) activities.

Secondly, language is a psychological function that mediates many other psychological competencies, such as perception, memory, cognition, social interaction, goal-directed behavior, just to list a few. Learning a new language is an inescapable part of being adopted internationally. From the psychological perspective, there are four major domains of direct language application: means of communication, behavior regulation, learning, and as a main medium of thinking/cognitive operations. Language is an effective psychological "tool" that addresses the consequences of early and ongoing trauma and forming social competences. It has multiple applications and must be considered in any therapeutic work and remedial programming for international adoptees.

Based on the above, it is understandable why The SmartStart Toolbox Program places such an emphasis on language-based activities. The language emphasis of the program may at first appear overwhelming for newly arrived international adoptees between the ages of four through eight, but this intensity is a necessary condition that transforms international adoptees into successful learners and communicators.

Language can be acquired in either a spontaneous and natural fashion, or it can be learned in a systematic and planned way, or it can be mastered as a combination of both. The internationally adopted children master their new language as a byproduct of living and sharing activities with native speakers. They do receive formal instruction in their new language at school, but teachers are only one source of language acquisition, whereas adoptive parents, peers, media, and culture at large are the most influential facilitators.

When adopted children enter an unknown cultural and linguistic environment, learning a language for them is no less than a survival skill. They have to acquire communicative language for normal functioning, as this mediates their entire process of adjustment. Thus, new language acquisition is the most crucial skill to be learned by internationally adopted children during their first year in an adoptive family (Gindis, 2019). The motivation to acquire the new language is much more intense in international adoptees than in bilingual children from immigrant families, as the adoptive family is the primary source of patterns of proper English, but not a sustained source of the native (first) language. A vast majority of internationally adopted children are not bilingual. They are monolingual on arrival and, after several months, they are again monolingual, but this time, with English. Therefore, internationally adopted children can be called "sequential" monolinguals, because, after a short period of transitional "bilingualism," they return to the status of monolinguals.

There are many ways to make language learning at home a more intense, cognitively enriching, and purposeful activity, while simultaneously keeping it a game-like fun pursuit that contributes to the attachment. These qualities are built into the activities of all units of The SmartStart Toolbox Program. Playing word games, reciting rhymes, and singing songs all help to build a sensitivity and awareness of the nuances of language that help to create "readiness" for reading. These experiences may in fact be much more relevant than drilling the child on alphabet and letter recognition. These actual reading skills will be much more likely to develop if the adopted child has a firm foundation in the language. If the child feels the mediator's enjoyment and shares the fun of interacting through language with the mediator, it will attach a positive emotion to these important learning opportunities. To further enhance language acquisition, we recommend the use of the following extra-linguistic supports:

- Gestures, facial expressions, regulation of loudness or tone of voice, body language, proxemics or personal space, eye gaze, touch, and other nonverbal means of communication to stimulate understanding.
- Repetition: try to repeat the same words several (or many) times in the context that is understood by the child.
- Use of pictures, artifacts, flashcards, and toys.

In conclusion, the basic principles discussed briefly above – "psychological tools" of cognition, mediated learning in the social context, emphasis on language, formation of attachment – are what we had in mind as we designed the specific activities for each unit of The SmartStart Toolbox Program.

Tips for Professionals Working Directly with Adopted Children or with Adoptive Parents

- We recommend that professionals create opportunities for the parents to meet in small groups (six to eight is ideal) on a weekly basis. Although it may restrict the number of people who are able or willing to commit to participation, we have found that six to eight sessions are necessary to get through the program and for the training experience to actually affect their behavior. We have also noticed that it takes about three sessions for the participants to begin to really relax and interact. Something seems to click at about the third session, and the participants are having more fun and doing more communication and exploration.

- We recommend three portions to each session: a review of the home-work from the previous unit (with a discussion about issues related to that); introduction of the new unit; hands-on activity from the new unit (materials will need to be provided and sent home with the participants. Of course, the first meeting would need to begin with an introduction to the whole program and an outline of how the workshop will proceed.

- Caregivers should be provided with some general ideas about the theoretical background and the goals of the program, and it should be emphasized (each time if necessary), that one goal is to promote their independent use of the ideas of the program.

- We also recommend that communication information be exchanged (with their permission) after completion of the program so that the exchange of ideas and support for their work with their children can continue. We haven't tried it yet, but it would also probably be a good idea to have occasional, well-spaced "booster" sessions to check on their progress and to secure feedback on their challenges and recommendations. Since the parents are encouraged to develop their own ideas, a newsletter to pass these on may also be interesting and helpful.

- Provision of (modest) refreshments is usually appreciated. If cost is an issue, the parents can be asked to contribute to the "kitty" to cover the cost of food and materials.

- Please use the SmartStart Toolbox: Workshop Program Evaluation (see the end of Chapter 3) to obtain feedback from the workshop participants.

References

American Psychiatric Association, DSM-5 Task Force. (2013). *Diagnostic and statistical manual of mental disorders: DSM-5™* (5th ed.). American Psychiatric Publishing, Inc. https://doi.org/10.1176/appi.books.9780890425596

Feuerstein, R., Hoffman, M.B. & Miller, R. (1980). *Instrumental enrichment.* Baltimore, MD: University Park Press.

Feuerstein, R., Rand, Y., Falik, L. & Feuerstein, R.A. (2003). *Dynamic assessment of cognitive modifiability.* Jerusalem: ICELP Press.

Gindis, B. (2019) *Child development mediated by trauma: The dark side of international adoption.* New York: Routledge.

Haywood, H.C. & Lidz, C.S. (2007). *Dynamic assessment in practice: Clinical and educational application.* New York: Cambridge University Press.

Lidz, C. & Gindis B. (2003). Dynamic assessment of the evolving cognitive functions in children. In A. Kozulin, B. Gindis, V. Ageev & S. Miller (Eds.), *Vygotsky's educational theory in cultural context* (pp. 99–116). New York: Cambridge University Press.

Rutter, M. (1999-A). Effects of qualities of early institutional care on cognitive attainment. *American Journal of Orthopsychiatry, 69*, 424–437.

Rutter, M. (1999-B). Resilience concepts and findings: Implications for family therapy. *Journal of Family Therapy, 21*(2), 119–144.

Vygotsky, L.S. (1987). *The collected works of L. S. Vygotsky: Problems of general psychology, including the volume thinking and speech*, Vol. 1; Vol. 2. The Collected Works of L.S.

Vygotsky, L.S. (1993). The collected works of L. S. Vygotsky. Volume 2: The fundamentals of defectology (abnormal psychology and learning disabilities). In R.W. Rieber & A.S. Carton (Eds.). (J.E. Knox & C.B. Stevens, Trans.). New York: Plenum.

Welsh, J.A., Viana, A.G., Petrill, S.A. & Mathias, M.D. (2007). Interventions for Internationally Adopted Children and Families: A Review of the Literature. *Child Adolescent Social Work Journal, 24*, 285–311.

3   Seven Units of The SmartStart Toolbox Program

This chapter contains the core of The SmartStart Toolbox Program: seven units of activities aimed at scaffolding learning and attachment in international adoptees. The seven units include: *Noticing Our World* (regulation of intentional attention and self-regulation in using senses), *Let's Make a Plan* (planning, organizing, and strategic problem-solving), *That's Fantastic* (fantasy and hypothetical thinking), *"The Nimble Symbol"* (understanding symbols as a representation and using symbols as a means of abstract reasoning), *What's the Big Idea?* (organizing and communicating information), *Who Is in Charge?* (self-regulation of attention, goal-directed behavior, movements, and expression of emotion), and *Making Connections to Strengthen Attachment* (building relationships within the family). Every unit starts with a succinct explication of its theoretical foundation and is followed by the psychoeducational objectives for each activity in the domains of cognitive skills, language proficiency, self-regulated behavior, and interpersonal relationships. The detailed description of activities includes recommendations for the parents and therapists about the needed materials ("Preparation" section) and the verbal instructions for guiding children through an activity (sections "What do I do?" and "What do I say?"). The wording for the activities is specifically adjusted for children who are still English learners and each unit ends with a vocabulary list of suggested words for mediators to use during the course of the activities. Language building and scaffolding are among major priorities of the program, along with the development of cognitive skills, self-regulated behavior and attachment. The units are designed to create and support connection and affection between newly adopted children and their adoptive parents through participation in joint/shared activities within positive emotional context. The activities

DOI: 10.4324/9781003253587-4

are selected or designed to be extensions of what parents would ordinarily do with their children, while using materials that are readily available. The units conclude with a brief survey titled "Mediator Response Questions" and the Chapter itself ends with a short "Workshop Program Evaluation."

UNIT 1. NOTICING OUR WORLD

Did You Ever Notice?
© C. S. Lidz
Did you ever notice
That leaves have different shapes?
And did you ever feel how dry
The skin can be on snakes?
Did you ever hear the tone of
Music from a drum?
And how it makes you
Stomp your feet and then
You start to hum?
Have you ever noticed
How sweet a peach can taste,
When picked right from a tree
And not gobbled up in haste?
There are many things to notice
If we only take the time
To look, and taste and touch and smell;
We make more moments shine.

Part 1. Learning How to Look, Listen, Touch and to Be Aware of the Surroundings

This Unit focuses on learning to use the senses to experience the environment: what and how to notice, how to talk about what is noticed, how to help a child to pay attention to patterns and sequences, and how to make groups based on perceived features. Ultimately, this Unit is primarily about regulation of intentional attention, a core ability to all that follows.

A Bit of Theory

Using the senses to take in stimuli is the most basic step in gathering information that serves as a foundation for thinking. Abstracting information from this database for use in detecting and creating patterns and for making comparisons are among the most basic and pervasive of higher mental processes. These processes are required for success with most early childhood and primary level curricula, and are essential for competence with more advanced academic demands as well as for general life skills: this is the foundation for abstract thought.

This unit is designed to help children learn what to notice when they use their senses. Just looking, touching, or tasting is not sufficient for building the database necessary for abstraction. Children need to be sensitized to the attributes and distinctive features of the stimuli to which they are exposed. They also need to develop a vocabulary for talking about these sensory experiences. In other words, mediation of these experiences is necessary.

Children who come from a disadvantaged background used to be described as stimulus-deprived and stimulus-overwhelmed. Such children were not able to discriminate among stimuli; theirs was a booming, buzzing, confusing world with little differentiation among all the available sights and sounds (Mackner, Starr, & Black, 1997).

For children from foreign orphanages, both the lack of stimuli and the lack of stimuli organization and mediation by adults are possible problems. Here is how an adoptive parent of an 8-year-old boy describes difficulties that arise from the imbalance in his early childhood stimulus processing experiences: "… it seems he has gaps, or what I describe as a lack of 'hooks' to put information on in his memory, making the next set of info nearly impossible to understand." This happens because a child who lived through a neglectful, impoverished institutionalization (orphanage) was deprived of an opportunity to learn to think. There was no particular adult in his life to serve as a model or to help to guide his thinking activities. There was no or very little of what we identify as a "mediated learning experience" in his life when an adult selects stimuli and organizes perceptions creating the foundation for higher thinking processes.

The Objectives of This Unit

- Learn to use our senses to experience the environment
- Develop a vocabulary to share our experiences
- Learn how to look and what to notice
- Detect the special features of what we experience
- Detect and produce patterns and sequences
- Make groups based on a shared characteristic
- To enhance the child's ability to regulate attention.

Activity 1: "What Is This?"

The goal: To help your child develop basic vocabulary and phrases to communicate with you and siblings at home and outside.

Preparation: Use any house object, toys, and lots of pictures from magazines to create flash cards.

What do I say? What do I do?

1   At the very beginning you will need to name basic things for your child and communicate to him/her what is expected, what are the rules of the house and how the child can convey what is needed from you.

2   Prepare pictures describing basic activities that you want your child to accomplish during the day and hang them on the wall in a row in the order you want them to be done. For example: getting up, taking shower, dressing, tooth brushing, making the bed, and so on.

3   You can select, cut out, and hang the pictures together with the child, while you explain briefly and name objects.

4   Repeat the same words several times in the context that is understood by the child.

5   Anticipate the needs of your child and what he/she may ask for ("I want to drink," "I want to eat," "I need to go to bathroom," etc.) and prepare cards with symbolic pictures and phases [addressed to you] to help your child indicate what may be needed.

6   Pick games that will help your child learn to name objects, colors, shapes, numbers.

Activity 2: "Details; Details ..."

The goal: To help your child tune into details of objects and develop a vocabulary for describing objects.

Preparation: Use any familiar object or toy in the home.

What do I say? What do I do?

1   Add details to the description of objects you ask for and talk about. For example: "Could you bring me the large pink plate please?" Or – "how about wearing your short-sleeved shirt with the blue and yellow stripes today?"

2   When your child asks for something, encourage him/her to use precise language. Don't just settle for "that one." Help your child by giving some choices, if your child doesn't have the vocabulary. For example, "You mean the large box with the big handle or the little box with no handle?"

3   Ask your child to describe the object using the word "and" to join the scripters. For example: "It is blue and shiny." Give your child two similar objects and encourage comparisons. For example: two cups – "this one is wider; this one is taller."

4   Draw "scribble pictures" with your child and describe what you have drawn. For example: "My scribble is orange and pointy and big."

5   Ask your child to say as many things as possible about a common object. Remind your child to use all the senses: how does it look? how does it feel? how does it smell? how does it taste? For example, a cup: "This is a cup. It is hard. It is shiny. It is blue. It can break. It is short. It has a handle. It is smooth."

6   Repeat this some more times and encourage your child to think of even more things. Keep a list, so you can show your child how many more were thought of. If your child has difficulty thinking of ideas, provide gestural cues by, for example, pointing to your eyes for "look," pointing to your nose for "smell," or pointing to the fingers of your opposite hand for "touch."

7   Set up a "tell me which one" game. Place two objects in front of you and your child. Take turns telling each other which one to pick. You have to use words that describe the object. For example: "Give me the one that is blue." Or – "Give me the one that is tall." This is a good way to practice vocabulary when your child is learning the new language.

8   Another version of this is to use edible items that your child can eat after providing the correct name and description, for example, the blue M&M or the long, thin pretzel. Be sure to make this fun so that it doesn't come across as a punitive way of having a snack!

Activity 3: "Sense-a-tional Food!"

(Children adopted from institutions may present mealtime challenges due to sensory (taste, smell, etc.) deprivation or over-stimulation. They may eat only a small range of foods, avoiding many other foods, refuse to sit and eat with the family at mealtimes, react negatively when presented with new foods, or insist on the same food at each mealtime).

The goal: To prepare your child's senses for mealtimes, help your child become more aware of what we notice with our senses during the food consumption, and how to use our senses to notice details of our experiences at mealtime.

Preparation: Regular mealtime food. This can take place during mealtime and/or while preparing food for a meal.

What do I say? What do I do?

1   Talk to your child during food preparation and feeding in terms of what you notice about the food. For example: "This apple is bright red. It must be ripe enough to eat." "These chips got wet; now they're soggy, and won't taste good."

2   Give your child choices that require noticing details. For example: "Do you want the dark, crisp fries, or the pale thick fries?" "Do you like the lettuce that has dark, pointy leaves, or soft, round leaves?"

3   Prepare some dish where your child can make some choices and describe the characteristics. For example: "Let's make some cookies. We'll each make them look different so we'll know who made them. Mine will be long and skinny. What will yours look like?" Or –

    Let's make some jello pudding and decide what to put in it. We'll take turns. For my turn, I want a pudding that is all green and has one thing that is juicy and one thing that is crunchy. What can I use? (How about some grapes for the juicy, and some celery for the crunchy?)

4   During mealtime, play a game of "I'm thinking of ..." For example, if you are eating a lunch of peanut butter and

jelly sandwich, glass of milk, and dish of peaches: "I'm thinking of something that is square and white [bread]," or – "I'm thinking of something that is juicy and orangey [peaches]."

5   Play "smell and tell" or "taste and tell" with different foods. Ask your child to close her/his eyes and see if she/he can tell you what the food is just by smelling, or tasting, or even touching.

6   Together with your child make a collage from magazine pictures of foods that share common characteristics. These could be foods that are crunchy, foods that taste sweet, foods that are red, etc.

Activity 4: "To See Is to Remember"

The goal: To help your child learn that noticing details helps us to remember.

Preparation: Storybook of interest to your child.

What do I say? What do I do?

1   Read a story to your child and point to the pictures as you read to help your child associate the picture with the story. Use your voice to make the story sound interesting and exciting. As you read through the story, point to the associated pictures and describe the details of the pictures as they relate to the story. As your child grows in language competence, pause to ask your child to find the picture that you described in the story (retell it to jog memory).

2   As you read through a story, cue your child to listen for a specific word, such as "bear." Tell your child, for example, to make a sound (growl) whenever she/he hears the word. Give your child a cue when you come to the word, such as pausing and looking at your child.

Part 2. Pattern Recognition and Pattern Production

Activity 1: "Cereal Serial"

The goal: To help your child notice and create patterns, and the ability to anticipate what comes "next" in a sequence based on a pattern.

Preparation: Mixture of leftover dry cereals of different shapes; paste, paper.

What do I say? What do I do?

1   Place small amounts of cereal with obviously different shapes in the child's bowl. Suggest to your child: "How about eating these in a pattern! Let's start with [for example] the round, then square, then round, then __?__." You can vary this and ask your child to decide how to start. You can increase and vary the pattern, for example, for "X Y X Y X Y …" or "X X Y X X Y" etc. Be sure to say the pattern for your child and then leave a blank and get your child to fill in the blank and anticipate what comes next. Work toward getting your child to initiate pattern ideas.

2   Use whole pieces of cereal to create patterns pasted on paper. Have cereal with varying shapes and colors. Begin with making a pattern and then asking your child to copy your pattern. Work toward having your child initiate original patterns. Start simply, with an X Y X Y idea, then build it up to be more challenging. See how many ways you can make patterns with the same materials.

3   Cereal with holes can also be used for making jewelry. Use a narrow shoelace and encourage your child to place the pieces on the string in a pattern. You can make the pattern first on the table and then place it on the string. Boys enjoy this as well as girls; if boys are uncomfortable, they can always make a necklace for Mommy. If this is too difficult to create from the start, ask your child to copy a pattern that you made, and encourage your child to say the name of each piece as the "beads" are placed on the string.

4   Look for patterns in your environment. The bathroom floor is one good place, building façades, another; wallpaper, clothing, etc. See if you can get your child to recognize patterns all around.

Activity 2: "A Moving Experience"

The goal: To help your child recognize that the body can make
    patterns with different movements.
Preparation: Just yourselves, and, later, a playground.

What do I say? What do I do?

1   While walking on the sidewalk, or up and down stairs, start
    saying to your child words to accompany movements, such as
    "up, up, up" or, counting, "one, two, three ..." or "left, right,
    left, right ..." Every once in a while get more playful, and
    suggest "hop, hop, hop ..." or "skip, skip, skip ..." or "hop,
    skip, hop, skip ..." When on the playground, suggest that you
    add a pattern to some of the activities, such as pushing the
    swing "strong, weak, strong, weak ..."
2   On the playground, suggest a game of placing or locating
    an object at some distance, for example, ten feet away. Suggest
    a game of thinking up how many different pattern ways you
    each can think of to reach that goal. For example, you could
    hop, skip, hop, skip, or, you could jump jump run jump jump
    run ... Take turns copying each other's patterns.
3   Try learning some dance steps that have patterns; play dance
    music and make up patterns, even if you don't know existing
    ones such as rumba or mambo.
4   Play a pattern movement game with hands, with each person
    thinking up a new pattern and asking the other person to
    copy it. For example, clap clap, pat (knees) pat (knees), touch
    (nose), clap clap ... You can do this with the whole family, with
    one person starting a pattern, and seeing how long it takes
    the rest to pick it up and start participating. (The pattern
    sequence should be repeated until everyone gets it, then start
    to increase the speed to see if you can get them mixed up).

Activity 3: "Pattern Pictures"

The goal: To help your child learn to create patterns.
Preparation: Crayons or markers and paper.

What do I say? What do I do?

1   Give your child one crayon and large paper and first observe
    what kinds of marks your child is able to make on the paper.

Try to find some words for these marks, such as "round," "line," "up line," "down line," "wave," etc. Then model using these marks to make a pattern, such as "up, down, up down" or "round, wave, round, wave ..."

2 With crayons and paper, encourage your child to fill up the whole page with different kinds of patterns. You could have a whole row of circles, then a row of scribbles, then a row of crosses. Then repeat these rows. Model the making of a "pattern page" for your child. You could first ask your child to name or draw some favorite shapes.

3 As you make the pattern, say the words that go with the marks. Try to get your child to copy your pattern and encourage your child to think of new ways to make marks so you can make patterns with these.

4 Help your child to notice the many patterns on clothing and home furnishings in your own home, as well as in others. Walk through a clothing or furnishings store on a "pattern hunt" to find as many patterns as possible. Which stores have the best patterns?

Part 3. Comparing and Classifying by Shape, Color, Size

Activity 1: "The Collector"

The goal: To help your child abstract characteristics of objects that place the object in a category or group.

Preparation: Any environment, indoors or outdoors.

What do I say? What do I do?

1 When shopping or preparing a meal, find times when you ask your child to "find another one, just like this." This is particularly easy in a grocery store, where you can pick one piece of fruit or vegetable and ask your child to find another one. Comment on what your child selects; for example: "that really does look like it, but yours has more bumps. Can you find one exactly the same?" This would work with sorting some clothing such as socks or looking for a lost shoe.

2 While taking a walk, decide to "collect" something. For example, during the fall, decide on a specific kind of leaf collection (for example, it must have two colors and be a whole

leaf). Analyze other things in the category to decide if it "fits" the collection. Talk with your child about the characteristics that make the new object fit or not fit in the collection. Sample things to collect: shells at the beach, pine cones from the park.

3   While walking or riding, suggest making a mental collection. For example, select a feature of an object such as the color green: "Let's collect the color green. Let's see how many green things we can find and who can find them first!" Encourage your child to come up with novel characteristics to "collect."

4   Talk to other children about their collections. Encourage your child to tell others about the collection and what the characteristics are of the pieces in the collection.

5   Visit a collection, for example, a museum. Pick something to focus on, such as pictures of children, and compare the pictures. How are they similar? How are they different? What are they trying to convey?

6   Play a mental collection game of "which things go together: a dog, a cat and what else?" Or, the variation on this: "which one doesn't belong? a dog, a TV, a cat, and a horse."

Activity 2: "I Spy"

The goal: To help your child develop a vocabulary for describing details noticed in the environment, and to help your child abstract important characteristics of these objects.

Preparation: Any environment, indoors or outdoors.

What do I say? What do I do?

1   Talk to your child as you put things away in terms of grouping them: "all the big towels here," "all the dark laundry here," "all the dinner plates here." "Sensitize your child to the groupings in your home and have your child help you divide things into groups."

2   Select three small objects from the environment. Place them in front of the child. Suggest a guessing game where one person gives a description and the other has to pick the one the describer is thinking about. You start as the leader, and use a function or category description, such as, for a cup: I

spy something we drink from, or, for a car, I spy something we ride in.

3   Play the "I Spy" guessing game. The point is to describe something in the room and the other person has to guess what it is. The person in charge (begin with you) first gives a broad category as a clue, then the child guesses. Each time the child misses the leader gives a more specific clue. For example, for a toy truck: first clue ("I spy something that rides."); second clue ("I spy something that rides and carries food to the market."); third clue ("I spy something that is red, that rides, and that carries food to the market.").

4   During activities such as walking or riding in the neighborhood, play the "I Spy" game. "I spy something that grows very tall. I spy something that is tall and brown; I spy something that is tall, brown, and has leaves."

Activity 3: "Pasta Sort"

The goal: To help your child notice characteristics of objects that make the object part of a group or category.
Preparation: Assorted leftover pasta pieces of varying shapes and colors (tricolor pasta would work best).

What do I say? What do I do?

1   Spill all the pieces of pasta together in one bowl and ask your child to sort them out into smaller bowls. Decide to have a "pasta sort" dinner and have your child ask each person what shape and color of pasta they would like.

2   With paper, paste, and pasta, encourage your child to create a picture with the various shapes. Talk about what is a good shape for what your child wants to put in the picture, and using a lot of the same shape if you want to fill in a space.

3   Plant a garden, either indoors or outdoors. Decide what to include and how to arrange them. Encourage creation of a pattern. Draw a sketch and try to get the garden to match the sketch.

Table 3.1 Vocabulary List for Unit 1: Noticing Our World

The words you use	*What the dictionary says*	*What you might say*
Notice	To refer to To pay attention To observe	Did you notice how cold it is today? Did you notice that I made you something special for breakfast? I notice that you look kind of tired.
Compare	To liken To examine for similarities and differences	Today is warm, compared to yesterday. Let's compare these shorts so you can decide what to wear.
Describe	To tell about	Describe to your dad what we did today. Let me describe what I saw in the store, and you tell me if you want it.
Pattern	A model or plan used in making things A regular way of acting or doing things	Your shirt has such an interesting pattern. Look how these pieces make a pattern. I notice a pattern to your behavior!
Sequence	The coming of one thing after another Order; series; result Result or consequence	What's the best sequence for making this? Let me show you the sequence of these dance steps.
Group	A number of persons or things gathered or classified together	Let's put these all in a group. Did you play by yourself or with your group?
Characteristic	A distinguishing trait or quality	You are really helpful; that's a very nice characteristic about you. This ketchup comes out too fast; that's characteristic of this brand.
Similar	Nearly, but not exactly the same or alike	Can you find some socks that are similar to your pants? These are similar, but not the same.
Different	Not the same or alike Distinct	This cake turned out to be different from the last one. Did you notice how different Jimmy looks? I feel like doing it a different way.

Source: Dictionary definitions are from Webster's New World Compact School and Office Dictionary (1982) by Simon & Schuster.

Unit 1: Mediator Response Questions for Noticing Our World

Parent's Name: Date:

Which activities did you do?

How did they go?

What modifications would you recommend?

Did you make up any activities relevant to the Unit's goals? What were these?

How did your child react while you worked on this Unit?

Any other comments?

UNIT 2. LET'S MAKE A PLAN

Planning
© C.S. Lidz
It helps to have a plan
When you have a lot to do.
You need to set a goal,
So your plan will see you through.
You start to work out steps
That all good plans involve
And think of a good strategy
For the problem that you solve.
You carry out your plan,
And then evaluate,
And finally you look back to fix
The parts that don't go straight.
You learn the words that guide
You from the start right to the end;
You smile when you are finished,
And then ... begin again!

A Bit of Theory

This unit focuses on connecting the present with the future by learning to think strategically, to set goals, to make a plan, to evaluate the results, and to make changes in response to this evaluation. The concepts of this unit form an essential basis for cooperation with others to achieve a goal, which contributes to formation of attachment between parents and their adopted children. The activities in this unit are also designed to help internationally adopted children develop skills related to self-regulation. Filled with family fun, the activities provide opportunities to engage children in prospective planning, understanding the sequence of steps involved, to enable completion of the plan, evaluate the effectiveness of the strategies, and make the adjustments and changes necessary to increase the effectiveness of the plan. All of these cognitive abilities are an integral part of successful school (and life) learning.

Making plans is a time when we can look into the future. Thinking about the future in adoptive family has a significant calming and therapeutic effect on the adopted child. It is very important for international adoptees to feel secure about the future with their new family, as most adoptees have a deep-seated and long-lasting fear of being sent back to their country of origin. Participation in short-term and long-term planning, anticipating when events begin and end, will have a positive psychological effect by diminishing their anxieties and improving their concentration and self-regulation.

Institutionalized children have very little control over what happens to them during their years in the orphanage. Right after the adoption they are unlikely to have developed the skills necessary for planning and evaluation. To facilitate this important aspect of their development, it is very important to plan **with** the child (**not for** the child) the beginning and the end of selected events throughout their day. Engaging them in these activities and approaches to thinking can help them develop confidence in their future and feelings of having some control over what happens to them in the future.

Helping your child to acquire the vocabulary necessary for planning (see vocabulary at the end of the unit) is another important step in your child's successful adjustment. Try to incorporate such words as "first, next, last, and previous" in your planning conversations.

Having a vision of the future and then being able to think through how to make that vision real are very important cognitive abilities (McGillicuddy-DeLisi, DeLisi, Flaugher, & Sigel, 1986). Talk with your child about that vision and try to help your child "see" as many details as possible. Where do you want to go? What do you want to do? How can we get there? What would happen if we did it this way or that way? These are all relevant questions.

Also, ask directly: "Do we need a plan? How did our plan work?" Work toward helping your child become a good planner and evaluator, someone who thinks strategically and is flexible enough to make changes when necessary. It is also a very good idea to model talking to yourself out loud about your own planning so that your child can hear all the different things that go into developing plans. This provides an important language model for your child. During these and other learning activities, try to use process-oriented vs. content-oriented questions, for example:

- Why do you think it's better to do it this way?
- What do you need to do next?
- What do you think would happen if _____?
- When have you done something like this before?
- When is another time you need to _____?
- Can you think of another way we could do this?

It's very important to reinforce the success of any plan that was accomplished. Speak about it with the child, pointing out that everything went so well because you had correctly calculated the time to get to the place ..., you had prepared the right clothes ..., you had looked up the road map ..., etc.

The Objectives of This Unit

- Learn to systematically explore and organize
- Think ahead about a goal
- Plan steps to reach the goal
- Determine if there is a necessary sequence
- Think about effective strategies
- Carry out the plan
- Evaluate how the plan worked
- Make changes to improve the plan

Part 1. Exploring and Organizing

Activity 1: "Important New Day"

The goal: To help your child explore a process of planning and develop the vocabulary for describing and evaluating plans.

Preparation: Find a place to go, preferably a place where you haven't been, and preferably one with lots of things to see and do. Bring paper or drawing board with crayons and markers for drawing the details of the trip (route, means of transportation, things to see, etc.)

What do I say? What do I do?

1   Before you go for a walk or a ride, talk about the best way to travel and what you need to take with you and think about before you go. For a bigger event choose the day and time for the trip well in advance. Check the weather, and ask your child to think about what is needed; for example: "It's going to be cold at that time; what do you think we should take with us?" Discuss the order of events with the child: "Why should we do this first?" If you're going to some place where you will stay for a while, ask your child what he or she would like to take along so there will be something to do; for example, plan to bring some game or toy if you are going on a long ride or going

---

to sit for a long time in a doctor's office. A good strategy for trip planning is to do a mental "walk" through the day: what will you need in the morning, afternoon, evening, nighttime? What will you need for the special activities you will do? What will you need for keeping busy during travel days?

2   Plan a visit to a department store or supermarket. Decide with your child how to explore and navigate around the area. Where will you start? Where do you want to end up? Do you notice anything about the plan of the store, such as the frozen food near the end, just before checking out? Talk about why certain things might be where they are and which things are grouped together. If you want to find something really fast, how would you do it?

3   Change your route riding or walking home. Which route is the best? What makes it the best? If you were going to tell someone how to get to your house (from?), what would you say? Explore your neighborhood. What is in front of your home? In back? To the right? To the left? Draw a picture of it.

Activity 2: "Object Hide and Seek"

The goal: To help your child learn to search systematically.
Preparation: A small toy or food.

What do I say? What do I do?

1   Place a small food such as a candy in one hand, close your hands, and have your child try to guess where it is. Establish a pattern, for example, alternating between right and left, and see if your child can figure out where it is. Tell your child that you are doing it according to a plan, and tell your child to try to figure out the plan. Remind your child of the pattern activities and to use this as a strategy for figuring out the plan.

2   Have your child close his or her eyes. Hide a toy or food treat in a designated room (tell your child which room). Encourage your child to search the room systematically; for example,

ask: "Where will you start? Let's do this according to a plan so you don't miss anything. It doesn't matter how fast we go. It only matters that we find it." Give your child a chance to do the hiding, and you talk aloud about how you will look for it.

3   Watch the child in the search activity above and then draw a picture of the pattern of his/her search. Were you systematic or trial and error?

4   When something gets lost, talk about how to think about finding it, such as retracing steps, remembering where you were last.

5   Do "walking" through the day – talk about what happened for the day and in which order. If you had a picture plan for the day, discuss if everything happened according to the plan or not. What accounted for the changes? Were they helpful or not? Were they controllable or not?

Activity 3: "Explore-a-toy"

The goal: To help your child find some new ways to enjoy a familiar toy through exploring new possibilities.

Preparation: Any familiar toy that doesn't have a "right" way to use it. A ball, crayon, blocks, play dough will do.

What do I say? What do I do?

1   Give your child a variety of toys and play with the child to make sure he or she knows how to use the toy. If the child uses it in a "babyish" way, for example, banging blocks, show how the blocks can be used for building.

2   With any common toy, such as a ball or clay, first let your child "mess with it" in whatever way first occurs. Then encourage your child: "let's think of something else to do with this." For example, if a ball was used for throwing, show how it could be used for rolling, kicking, hitting, aiming at a target. See how many things you can do with one "simple" play object.

3   Using a construction toy, let your child build whatever comes to mind first. Then encourage your child to "do it another way." Help your child to see different ways to use the materials, for example, if long pieces were all standing up, show how they could be used lying down.

4   If your child does something troublesome, talk in terms of "What else can you do? Is there another way?" Ask: what were you trying to accomplish? What's the best way to do that?

5   Help your child think of all the different ways some foods can be prepared, such as changing what goes into a fruit salad, or the ingredients for pizza. Think of all the ways something can be changed and still be that thing. Is it still a pizza if it's square? How about shaped like a triangle?

Activity 4: "I've Got to Get Organized"

The goal: To help your child organize their own living and playing spaces.

Preparation: Paper and pencil, as well as boxes and/or shelving for placement of clothes and play items.

What do I say? What do I do?

1   Take your child on a walking tour of the bedroom and play area and talk the child through where things are kept, why (when relevant), and where they should go when not being used.

2   Have your child work with you to sort the laundry and place it where it belongs and, also, to clean up the play area when finished, to return items to where they belong. Talk your child through these clean up times, and sing a little clean up song to go along with it.

3   Write labels and draw picture clues to indicate where objects and clothing belong and place these on edges that can be seen clearly by your child.

Part 2. Setting Goals; Thinking About Strategies; Making and Carrying Out a Plan; Evaluating and Adjusting the Plan

---

Activity 1: "I'm Puzzled"

The goal: To help your child think about the end result and how to get there.

Preparation: A multipiece puzzle, or you can make your own by selecting a picture from a magazine, cutting it up and pasting it on cardboard.

What do I say? What do I do?

1   With a simple inset puzzle, help your child get the idea of placing pieces where they belong. Help your child notice the clues that help. Talk about turning the pieces the right way, looking for clues for where the pieces belong, as well as for judging if they are in the right place.

2   With a multipiece inset puzzle, talk about a plan for doing puzzles; for example, looking at the whole picture before it is messed up, turning all the pieces right side up, doing the easy, most obvious pieces first (and noting what clues make it easy), using other cues such as color matching. Try different types of puzzles with the content matching, color or shape matching, or combination of the above.

3   When working on any multipiece game, such as a construction toy, talk with your child about helpful strategies and clues to notice. Encourage your child to make a mental picture of what they want it to look like. They can make whatever changes they like along the way, but they should try to have a goal/vision in mind.

Activity 2: "Kitchen Capers"

The goal: To help your child think ahead, make a plan, and carry it out.

Preparation: Any recipe for cooking.

What do I say? What do I do?

1   Select a simple cooked dish that the child likes. Talk about the ingredients: what do we need? Do we have it at home? Do we need to buy it? What happens if we use this ____ instead

of that? Go to the supermarket to choose the necessary ingredients. After cooking is finished, ask: "How did we do?", "Is there any way we could make this even better next time?"

2   Select a multistep recipe that you think will be do-able with your child. Talk through gathering the right ingredients, and what to do first, next, last. Talk about what is a necessary versus not necessary sequence; for example, "does it matter if we do this ___ before this? What would happen if we did ___ first?"

3   Let your child be responsible for setting up the table. Help your child think in terms of the sequence of the meal, what utensils are needed for each dish, where they go, what kind of table decoration will be appropriate. When the meal is finished, chat with your child about how it went; what went well, what could be done better next time.

4   Help make your child aware of the organization of your kitchen (assuming it is!), while naming things, let your child think through with you where things should go and be stored. For example, why this egg has to be stored in the refrigerator and that jar of salt should be stored in the pantry?

Activity 3: "Getting to Know You"

The goal: To help your child plan a social event.
Preparation: Invite a friend or friends of your child for any occasion.

What do I say? What do I do?

1   Ask your child who would be a good friend to invite over for a play date, and talk to your child about "when" this could happen, "where" it can be (for example, at home, in the playground), "what" they might do, and what steps you have to take to make it happen (for example: "I'll need to call Tommy's mom to find out if he can come here on Saturday to play with you."). Let your child listen to you making the arrangement and tell your child the results of the conversation.

2   Help your child invite a friend over to play, and help your child get some play props ready for the friend. Have your

child help you think through what might be a good snack to have with the friend. After the occasion, talk with your child about how it went: what the friend seemed to enjoy the most; what could have gone better; what to think about next time.

3   Help your child be aware of other people's plans, for example, when there is a field trip in school, talk about all the different steps involved in the event, or if your child goes to someone else's home to play or for a party, talk about all the different things that were involved.

4   For a special occasion (for example, a birthday), plan a party with several children that includes a sequence of several activities. Work with your child to think through whom to invite, what to do with them, what to feed them, what you need to buy and prepare, what the best sequence will be. Prepare some "crib sheet" for reference as a checklist. Let your child shop with you and help you set it up. Talk with your child after the event to evaluate how it went. What was the best part and the most fun? Were there any glitches?

Activity 4: "Home Theatre"

The goal: To help your child plan a "theatrical" event.
Preparation: Some good ideas and props for whatever these ideas generate.

What do I say? What do I do?

1   Take turns with your child, acting out what each of you tells the other to present. For example, you tell your child to act out "a dog" and your child tells you to act out "a clown." Once you get this going, build in some silly mistakes, such as making the dog say "meow," and ask your child "did I do anything wrong? what's the silly thing?"

2   Divide up a large sheet of blank paper into several sections, for example four. Encourage your child to "draw the story you just saw." Help your child think through the sequence of a story on TV or in the movies and draw the story sequence.

"Let's see if we can tell this story in just four pictures. What happened first, right at the beginning; then what happened next and next, and then what happened at the end?" (Don't worry about the quality of the art. Any representational symbol will do as long as you share the meaning).

3   Use some puppets or stick figures to act out a familiar story with your child. Work with your child to set this up and to assign roles. Afterward, look back at the story to see if anything important was left out.

4   Help your child develop an original story/play to be performed for friends or family (if this is hard for your child, this can be "borrowed" from one your child already knows by just changing some elements in the story). This might involve other children to take parts. Help your child first develop the story and then think through how it can be presented. Let your child be the "director" and tell all the "actors" what to do. You might want to make a storyboard to help the actors remember the sequence of the story.

Activity 5: "Planned TV Watching (or, Who's in Control of This, Anyway?)"

The goal: To help your child think ahead about what TV shows to watch, and to give you ultimate control over your child's TV watching.

Preparation: TV program guide.

What do I say? What do I do?

1   Talk about some rules for watching TV. Help your child choose a TV program. Give your child a controlled choice (this or that) and some rule about TV watching, such as "just two shows this evening." Parents get the last word on the plan. Be sure to turn the TV off once the family plan is realized. Keep the ultimate decision-making in your hands (resort to "because I said so," if necessary).

Table 3.2 Vocabulary list for Unit 2: Let's Make a Plan

The words you use	What the dictionary says	What you might say
Plan	A diagram showing the arrangement of something; A scheme for making, doing, or arranging something	This is pretty complicated; I think we need a plan. What steps do we need for our plan? So, how did our plan work out?
Prepare	Get ready; to make ready; to equip; to furnish; to put together	Let's prepare to make our dinner. Are you prepared to go to the party?
Explore	To examine something carefully; To investigate; to travel in a little known region for discovery	Let's explore all the different ways we can do this. When we go to a new place, it's fun to explore.
Evaluate	To find the value or amount; appraise	We'd better evaluate what happened here.
Goal	The place at which a trip ends; Objective	Before we start, let's think about our goal.
Strategy	The science of planning; a plan or action; skill in managing or planning.	We need a good strategy to make our plan work.
Future	That is to be or come; the time that is to come	Let's make a plan for the future.

Source: Dictionary definitions are from Webster's New World Compact School and Office Dictionary (1982) by Simon & Schuster.

Unit 2: Mediator Response Questions for Let's Make a Plan

Parent's Name: Date:

Which activities did you do?

How did they go?

What modifications would you recommend?

Did you make up any activities relevant to the Unit's goals? What were these?

How did your child react while you worked on this Unit?

Any other comments?

UNIT 3. THAT'S FANTASTIC!

Imagination
© C.S. Lidz
Imagine this: you're in a tree;
There's chirping all around.
You spread your wings,
And make a nest
From twigs found on the ground.
Imagine now that you're an ant,
Or something else real small.
You eat up crumbs (or food that's worse),
From picnics in the fall.
Or, be a car, with four big wheels
That whirl around real fast,
With motor noise that sounds so loud
When you start off with a blast.
What else can you imagine
If you think about it now?
What would it be like if you were born
A monkey or a cow?

This unit focuses on developing imagination, as well as divergent, and hypothetical thinking. Children are encouraged to make "what if?" speculations and to entertain strange combinations and alternative approaches. This unit helps adoptive parents to unleash the creativity inherent in their children and to help give direction to this creativity. So, this is an opportunity to put a damper on the evaluation skills developed in the previous Unit. This is a chance to "go with the flow," and, "short of actual danger," "let it all hang out."

A Bit of Theory

Fantasy is not only entertaining, but also it allows us to rehearse, set goals, self-motivate, escape, reduce stress, and self-regulate. Fantasy combined with talent, skill, and training can lead to creation of stories, visual art, music, poetry, and dance. But skill and talent are not prerequisites for fantasy. Anyone can engage in this mental activity. Development of imagination allows us to move backward and forward in time, and keeps us from being bound to what we can see and touch in the here and now. Imagination is the basis for invention, prediction, and fun and provides an important foundation for the development of abstract thinking.

For children, fantasy comes naturally and is just plain fun. However, play skills in children raised in an institution have long been a matter of concern for adoptive parents and professionals working with international adoptees (Rutter, 1999-B). Thus, it was reported in a book written by a group of Russian psychologists, that children at Russian orphanages between the ages of two and six were delayed, rather profoundly, in their abilities to play with toys, to play independently, to be involved in an imaginary play, and, later, in play with other children (Gindis, 2019). This means that adoptive parents will need to facilitate and develop play skills and imagination in their children in order to remediate the lack of play skills as a consequence of their child's past. Play, particularly imaginary (dramatic) play, and joint/shared play with an adult or older or more advanced peer, is the most effective and powerful tool we can give to adopted children to help them master the English language. In normal childhood development, play is intrinsically motivated. It is based on the pleasure involved in motion, fantasy, competition, etc. For internationally adopted children who may experience delays in their development of play skills, at least part of their play needs to be externally motivated, stimulated by their caregivers and more advanced peers.

This is also a time when it is important to help your child distinguish between reality and fantasy. Talk to your child about what is real and imagined; help your child understand that experiences such as stories on TV are only made-up stories from someone else's imagination and that there is a difference between "news" and fiction. Join and encourage your child's imaginative ideas; don't be afraid of fantasy, but, instead, have fun with it together. Build some castles in the air! Select reading material and videos that will let your child use imagination to help solve childhood concerns and stresses. Use words like: "what if …" and "what do you think will happen?"; "what else could you do?" Once your child has offered a solution or completed a task, ask "what's another way this could be done?" or, "Can we think of something else that might work?" Find opportunities to encourage your child to make predictions of what "might" happen.

The Objectives of This Unit

* Differentiate between real and imagined
* Appreciate the importance of imagination and fantasy
* Develop hypothetical thinking
* Think of alternatives
* Make predictions

Part 1. Fanciful Thinking

Activity 1: "Cloud Nine"

The goal: To encourage your child to use imagination, fantasy, and flexible thinking with cloud "pictures."
Preparation: Go outdoors on a cloudy day, preferably with lots of cumulus (puffy) clouds.

What do I say? What do I do?

Look up at the clouds with your child. Find some cloud that looks like something to you and tell your child what you see. Point to another cloud and ask your child what that one could be. Do some more, as long as this holds your child's interest. Share your own ideas and model by focusing your child's attention at times on smaller parts, at times on larger, at times on cloud combinations. Younger children will see simpler, single pictures, such as a "clown" or a "dog." As children develop and acquire richer vocabulary, they become more capable of seeing and relating complex stories and pictures that interact ("a boy reading a book," "a cat chasing a mouse").

Activity 2: "Play Time!"

The goal: To support your child's use of fantasy in play and use of play to develop fantasy
Preparation: Any set of toys that can create a theme, such as a doll family, a farm or home setting.

What do I say? What do I do?

1   Encourage your child to play thematic games with the toys and household objects in the house: "In the airport," "In the supermarket," "In the school," "At the doctors," etc., imagining being a pilot, a doctor, or a teacher and transforming toys into the necessary props. Take a role of someone who is interested, watching, and describing, but not directing. Encourage your child to interact with the toys and just add enough to help the flow of the action or conversation. If your child talks while playing, you can merely listen and be an appreciative audience

or enter into a dialogue on behalf of your own character. If your child doesn't talk and just moves the pieces, you supply the words and just describe what your child does ("the girl walks up to her mom; her mom gives her a cup; they sit at the table ..."). If your child wants you to take more of an active part, encourage your child to "be the director," and you follow your child's lead. Be sure not to make any evaluative comments, except perhaps at the end to say something like "that was fun!"

2   With construction toys such as blocks, legos, bristle blocks, "construct a dream" with your child by suggesting your child make a dream house or a dream playground or a dream school, or whatever you think might spark your child's interest.

Activity 3: "If I Were ..."

The goal: To help your child think beyond "what is" to "what could be" by considering what it would be like to be something or someone else.

Preparation: No preparation.

What do I say? What do I do?

1   Play the "if you were an animal" game by suggesting to each other (the rest of the family can do this with you): "If you were an animal, how would you talk and how would you move?" Take turns telling the person next to you (decide whether you're moving to the right or left) which animal to imitate, and say the phrase to that person: "If you were an elephant how would you talk? How would you move?"

2   Encourage your child to think of what it would be like to be someone or something else. Get your child to select someone or something else to be and to tell you what that might be like; write down what your child says and ask your child to draw a picture of what that might be like. For example, what would it be like to be an ant in your backyard? What would it be like to be your sister or brother? What would it be like to be your car or your TV?

3   Give your child a stick to serve as a "magic wand." Tell your child that she or he can pretend that this magic wand can

make anything change. For example, this magic wand can turn spinach into chocolate cake! Go around outside with your child, playing with making as many changes as your child wishes. Let your child keep the wand handy to make any changes that may catch her or his imagination. Be sure not to evaluate any of the "changes" (as long as these are kept imaginary), but join your child in the fun and perhaps make a wand for yourself.

Activity 4: "Make 'em' and Bake 'em'"

The goal: To develop fanciful exploration using a cooking activity.
Preparation: A simple cookie dough preparation, either ready-made from the freezer department of the supermarket, or from scratch from your favorite recipe book.

What do I say? What do I do?

1   Put blobs of cookie dough onto a cookie sheet before cooking. Encourage your child to "see" pictures in the dough; begin by making your own suggestions ("Look! doesn't that look like a dog's face?").
2   Divide the cookie dough into individually sized portions. Help your child think of weird animals and monsters to make with the dough and help your child form the shapes. Do this by hand and not with a cookie cutter. Add M&M's, or other trimmings to make the appearance more interesting and colorful.

Activity 5: "Blotter Blobs"

The goal: To help your child think ahead and make predictions of what a blotter picture will look like.
Preparation: Plain paper that will absorb paint, and choices of different washable colors of paint.

What do I say? What do I do?

1   Show your child how to make a blotter picture by folding a paper (for example, 8 1/2 by 11 inch) in half to create a crease. Then open it up and place a few dabs of paint right in the center on the crease. Next, fold the paper and press the two

sides together to get the paint to spread. Then open it up to view the results. Help your child appreciate the attractiveness of the result and the fun of turning dabs into a pretty picture.

2   Do the blotter picture as described in activity 1, but help your child think ahead about how she or he wants the picture to look. Which colors will you use? Where will you put each? Ask your child to try to imagine how it will look when opened up.

3   Do as above, but increasing the number of color choices and the complexity of the pictures. Ask your child to tell what the picture looks like when opened up, and "what else" it could be. Get your child to predict what the picture will look like before opening the paper and evaluate how close the picture came to the prediction.

4   Instead of paper you can use a piece of plastic or any other polished surface. Drop several dabs of paint on the surface. Put a piece of paper that does not absorb paint easily (printer paper will do) on top of it and smooth it out over the painted surface. Then lift this piece of paper from the surface. Depending on how you do it: lifting it straight up, or pulling down or pulling sideways, there will be a new "landscape" on the paper. Change paint and paper colors and the way you pull the paper off the surface to come up with a great variety of different images. Ask your child to describe what he/she can see in the colorful abstract images you just created together.

Part 2. Making Inferences and Predictions

Activity 1: "What if ...?"

The goal: To help your child speculate about the effects of changes.
Preparation: No preparation.

What do I say? What do I do?

1   Get your child to think about "what if ..." changes in things with which your child is very familiar.

Pose questions such as: "What if ...

- all we had to eat were ice cream?"
- we had no cars?"
- you couldn't talk?"
- we ate dessert first?"
- you woke up and were suddenly a teenager?"
- we lived in the city/country?"
- we had daytime all the time and no nighttime?"
- you had a magic genii who got you anything you wanted?"

Activity 2: "Change the Story"

The goal: To sensitize your child to the fact that stories in books and on TV are imaginary, and to help your child have the experience of controlling the imaginary events of a story.

Preparation: A book that your child is familiar with or a story you have both watched on TV.

What do I say? What do I do?

1   Read through a simple story with which your child is familiar. Then suggest telling the story again, but with a different main character. For example, change a fox into a bear or a caterpillar into a lion.

2   Read through a familiar story with your child, but, before it ends, stop, and ask your child to make up a new and different ending. You might need to do this once or twice yourself to show how to make the change, since this will seem quite strange to your child.

3   As you read a new story with your child, stop periodically and ask: "why do you think they did that" or "why do you think that happened?" Then, as you have enough information and near the end, ask: "What do you think will happen?"

4   Go through a familiar story with your child, and encourage your child to retell the story from another point of view. For example, there is an entertaining book on the market that retells the story of the "Three Little Pigs" from the point of view of the wolf, and another that speculates: "what if there were four little pigs?"

Table 3.3 Vocabulary list for Unit 3: That's Fantastic!

The words you use	What the dictionary says	What you might say
Imagination	The act of forming mental images of what is not present; The act or power of creating new ideas by combining previous experiences	What do you imagine it would be like? You have a very vivid imagination.
Hypothesis	An unproved theory tentatively accepted to explain certain facts	Your hypothesis is that you'll never be sad again if I buy that for you?
Think	To form or have in the mind; To use the mind; Reflect; Reason	Let's stop for a minute and think before we act. Sometimes thinking about it keeps us from making a mistake.
Predict	To state what one believes will happen; Foretell	Can you predict what will happen next? I bet you didn't predict that!
Alternative	Providing a choice between things	There's got to be another alternative. Stop that and think of an alternative. What else could you do?
Create	Bring into being; Originate; Invent; Design	Let's create our own idea for a costume. That will really create a mess!
Real	Existing as or in fact; Actual; genuine	I'm not kidding. This is real and not imagination. My dream seemed real.

Source: Dictionary definitions are from Webster's New World Compact School and Office Dictionary (1982) by Simon & Schuster.

Unit 3: SmartStart Toolbox Mediator Response Questions for That's Fantastic!

Parent's Name: Date:

Which activities did you do?

How did they go?

What modifications would you recommend?

Did you make up any activities relevant to the Unit's goals? What were these?

How did your child react while you worked on this Unit?

Any other comments?

UNIT 4. THE NIMBLE SYMBOL

Symbols
© C.S. Lidz
A red heart means "love"
A green light means "go";
A line through a circle
Means "no."
A fork says "let's eat";
The clock says "you're late";
Some arrows point up;
Some "straight."
A symbol is something
All people can read
Without even knowing a word.
But letters and numbers
Are all symbols too
To make sure that your thoughts
Can be heard.

This unit directly addresses the use of symbols in our environment and focuses on laying a foundation for emerging literacy and numeracy.

A Bit of Theory

We live in a symbol-using culture. Children need to learn to use symbols in order to adapt successfully to our high-tech world. Using money; telling time; reading and make math calculations; understanding advertisement, and on and on – these all involve symbols. Symbols give us freedom and let our minds roam far beyond what we can see, hear, and touch. Symbols play a critical role in learning.

Although in this unit we deal most directly with the content areas of reading and mathematics, we, however, made the decision not to use the actual content, but to focus on underlying processes and "readiness" types of foundation skills. We assume that any school program will teach children the alphabet, word recognition, and numerical operations, but not every program will provide adequate preparation for learning the foundation skills offered here.

The research evidence is very strong in identifying phonemic awareness as a basic and important foundation skill for reading. Because reading and math are symbol systems, we felt it was necessary for children to "get" the idea of symbols across a variety of contexts.

This should give them more in-depth understanding of the arbitrariness of letters, words, and numbers, and, we hope, give them a better sense of control as they go about mastering these challenging tasks.

The activities that involve symbol manipulation are an intrinsic part of family's life, although parents often do not realize that the activities they share with their children (talking, drawing pictures, engaging in pretend play, visiting places, etc.) carry a lot of symbolic substance (Zambrana-Ortiz & Lidz, 1995). In these activities, children sometimes learn through direct explanation: "Do you see this picture? It means hot, so do not touch it," but more often they learn through imitation. Children can observe their parent's reactions to certain symbols, for example: a parent does not cross the street when the sign "Do Not Walk" is on, and learn the symbolic nature of our world.

A different picture is observed with children raised in institutions, especially if orphanage placement was preceded by life in a neglectful and abusive family. In such families minimal, if any of the adults' mediation is given to symbolic matters. The children may have had no experience with symbols, and the whole concept of symbol may be foreign to them. Adoptive parents in most cases should not make any assumptions and work consciously to create awareness of symbols in their children, and to develop their ability to manipulate and create symbols.

Bring your adopted child's attention to the symbols in your environment. Talk to your child about what these symbols mean. Talk about how symbols can make life more interesting and more productive/effective, for example, using a picture to portray a complex idea (another good opportunity for "what if" thinking; "what if we didn't have this symbol?"). Extend the Imagination Unit into this one to ask the child to improve the symbol, to make a different one, even a crazier, funny one. Extend the Planning Unit into this one to ask your child to evaluate the effectiveness and appropriateness of the symbol. What would make it better?

The Objectives of This Unit

- Recognize the existence of symbols
- Develop the ability to create symbols
- Develop the ability to use symbols
- Develop positive attitude and readiness for literacy

Part 1. Recognizing Symbols

Activity 1: "Signs of the Times"

The goal: To increase your child's awareness of the symbols in our environment and how we use symbols to "represent" something.

Preparation: Walk or drive to a place that has signs.

What do I say? What do I do?

1   Take a "symbol walk or drive" around your neighborhood. See how many signs and symbols you can find. Traffic signs, religious symbols, advertising; these can be pointed out and talked about. These can also be classified into groups such as "religion" or "directions" or "feelings" (for example, hearts for "love"). Look around your house, for example, in your medicine cabinet or your food shelves for symbols; do you find symbols for prescription? poison? what else? Explain to your child that symbols are "reminders"; they are a way to make us pay attention, or help us remember, or help us think about things that we can't see.

2   Be on the alert for symbols in ads in TV commercials.

3   What do these small signs on the remote controls of your TV, or VCR, or DVD mean?

4   Take any computer game. There will be always a lot of signs used in the game for manipulation and control. What do these signs mean? Try to figure it out together with your child.

5   Pick up a geographic map or a road atlas and pretend that your family is going to drive to Disney Land for a vacation. What are these road map signs telling us? Are we going to get there in a week or in a day?

Part 2. Creating Symbols

Activity 1: "My Secret Language"

The goal: To help your child experience the use of an alternative means of communication by using gestures to represent what would otherwise be said with words.

Preparation: No preparation.

What do I say? What do I do?

1   With your child, decide to use gestures that will have special meaning for you both. For example, gestures that will signal when you want to be left alone, or when you are hungry, or when you need a hug. Use these gestures as your special way of communicating. This may be especially helpful when you are with "company" or out in public and you want to tell your child something without embarrassment.

2   Bring your child's attention to deaf people who are communicating with sign language and explain how those signs are their way of talking. Try to figure out what some of the signs could mean just from their appearance.

Activity 2: "Symbols in My Home"

The goal: To learn to create symbols for common areas within your home. To develop the ability to represent a category with a single concept.

Preparation: Think about how things in your house are organized (or not). You will need some paper and crayons or paint, or you could cut pictures out of a magazine and paste them on paper.

What do I say? What do I do?

1   With your child, look at areas of your house, beginning with your child's room, and think about which groups of objects go together. Create a symbol for each and place this on a paper as a sign for that area. Help your child think of an idea that can be portrayed as a symbol for that area. Have fun with this and get silly, but try to make the idea relate to the category represented. For example, your child might want to use a "poison" (skull and crossbones) sign for a private toy area as a warning for others not to disturb. If your child has difficulty thinking of ideas, you could offer a choice of two or three and have your child make a choice. Then help your child draw the picture for the idea.

Activity 3: "Our Family Shield"

The goal: To help your child understand the relationship between a symbol and the "thing" it represents through making personal symbols and symbols for the family.

Preparation: Paper, colored pencils, markers, or paint for drawing.

What do I say? What do I do?

1 Introduce your child to the idea of a shield as something that people did a long time ago to show others who they were and to pass down to their children. You might be able to find a storybook that shows how shields were used.

2 Think of things that are special for your family, and think about how that could be represented by a picture or other kind of symbol. Make a family shield and use this for special events like signing greeting cards or as a decoration for a party. You may have to start by giving your child some ideas and showing how these can be placed onto a shield. Encourage your child to talk about the shield to visitors and with teachers and children in the child care program.

3 Have each person in your family decide on a special symbol for themselves. You could combine each of these symbols into your family shield.

Part 3. Using Symbols

Activity 1: "Ready, Set, Read"

The goal: To familiarize your child with books as a source of fun and information.

Preparation: Any book that you think will interest your child and that is geared for your child's age level.

What do I say? What do I do?

1 Read stories to your child and run your finger along the sentences to show that the words determine what you say. Seat your child so that you are both looking at the pages together. Acquaint your child with the need to turn the pages one by one, to start at one end and progress to the other. Ask your

child to find the picture for what you are reading. Use your voice to create interest and excitement in the story. Read through to the end without too much stop and start, but be sure the selection is short enough to keep your child's interest.

2   Help your child make up a storybook by stapling blank pages together. Help your child tell the story of his or her day or about a special experience such as a trip to the zoo. You can write out the story that your child makes up, and your child can draw a picture on each page.

3   Let your child make decisions about what is read. Encourage your child to make mental pictures for the reading content and not just rely on the pictures in the book. Let your child do "pretend reading" of a familiar story to you. Before reading a new story, first talk about what your child already knows about the subject matter of the story. After the story is finished, talk about it – about what was interesting, about what was hard to understand, about inferences that could be made. Encourage your child to talk about what you are reading with others. Help your child become aware that stories usually have a beginning, a middle, and an end.

Activity 2: "Family Fun"

The goal: To represent family members with symbols and to learn that symbols are invented and can change.

Preparation: A variety of materials that can be divided up to represent people in a family.

What do I say? What do I do?

1   Use a variety of materials to "make a family." This can be done with materials such as playdoh, sticks, blocks, pretzels, coins, and so on. Suggest to your child that you use the materials to make a family. Ask who will be in the family. Then decide with your child how each family member will be represented. Then think of different ways of making a family, such as: "let's make a round family"; or, "let's make a flat family." Ask your child "what's another way we can make a family?" (With

younger children, you would need to be more "concrete" and perhaps use dolls or animals or candies that look like people or animals. As the children get older, it is possible to be more abstract and have a stick or block family.)

2   Encourage your child to use materials symbolically during play, for example, during doll play, if there is no actual toy food, suggest pretending that something else "represent" the food.

Activity 3: "Measure for Pleasure"

The goal: To develop an understanding of measurement and the need to use something smaller than the thing that is measured.

Preparation: A large object to measure.

What do I say? What do I do?

1   Introduce concepts of "big," "little," "small," "tall," "short," "long," "more," "less." Use these words when you can, for example, when serving food.

2   Suggest playing a "measuring game." This game is to decide all the different ways something can be measured. Pick something in your house to measure, for instance, a piece of furniture. Give an example, such as "See this table? I can measure it with my hands. Let us see how many hands long it is! Now, I think I'll measure it with this pencil. Let's see how many pencils it is!" Then ask your child to pick something to use for measuring, and, once done, to think of another way to measure the same thing.

3   Once you have measured the object at least two different ways, you can ask questions such as: is the table more hands or pencils? You can also expand on this activity with ideas such as: go find something that is two pencils long.

4   When you have measured something, introduce the idea of keeping track of how many things it is by using slashes for each number, as in Roman numerals. Once this becomes cumbersome, introduce the idea of Arabic numerals as an easier and more efficient way to keep record.

Activity 4: "It's About Rhyme"

The goal: To sensitize your child to the sounds of language.
Preparation: Poems and songs that rhyme.

What do I say? What do I do?

1   Rhymes are an excellent way to make children aware of the sounds of language. Find a good book of rhymes, and read these over and over to your child. Use your voice to emphasize the sounds that rhyme. (It's even OK to use the rhymes provided here!).

2   Once the child has heard the rhyme, try stopping before the end of a line and let your child finish the phrase.

3   Play a rhyme game by picking a word and challenging your child to think of words that rhyme with it; give your child a chance to pick words for you to rhyme. You could make this more advanced by rhyming within categories, for example: "Think of a color that rhymes with bread!"

Activity 5: "Because I Said so!"

The goal: To encourage good listening and following of directions.
Preparation Experience with "Simon Says" game.

What do I say? What do I do?

1   Children always enjoy the chance to give orders and to be in charge, especially if they can boss an adult around. This is a version of "Simon Says" that can be called "Teacher Says," "Mommy Says," or "Daddy Says," or whatever you and your child decide. The idea is to give directions to the other person (or people). The directions can vary by length, beginning with one thing to do at a time, graduating to two and three things to do at a time. For the beginner, you would need to provide some examples, and to be sure that you give only one short, easy-to-follow direction. Try to make it fun and do some silly things, such as "touch your nose with your tongue," or "tickle your tummy ..." For the more experienced child, directions can become more complex, for example: "Teacher says: stand up, put your hand over your mouth, and hop on one foot."

2   To promote good listening and create more challenge, this game can also be done just as the traditional "Simon Says," where the listener only follows directions preceded by "Simon (or whomever) Says."

3   This is quite challenging, but fun. Take several index cards and draw a simple design on each. Then take turns being "teller" and "listener." The "teller" selects a card and has to tell the "listener" what to draw; the listener can't look at the card, but can only draw what the teller says. At the end, compare the drawings. For example, "draw a blue dot in the top middle of the card and a red square in the bottom middle," or, "draw a small black circle inside a large red square." (Adjust the complexity to suit your child).

Table 3.4 Vocabulary list for Unit 4: The Nimble Symbol

The words you use	What the dictionary says	What you might say
Symbol	A thing that represents another; A written or printed mark, letter, etc. standing for a quality or process	This is a symbol of my love. Written words are symbols of what we say when we talk or think.
Number	A symbol or word showing how many or which one in a series	We need to buy the right number for our party. Count the people, and we'll write the number right here.
Letter	Any character of the alphabet	First you have to learn the names and sounds of the letters. The letters have to go in a certain order or you can't read them.
Represent	To be a symbol for	This book represents the day you were born. I'll bring home this stone to represent this trip.
Read	To get the meaning of writing by interpreting the characters	I'll read you a story before you go to sleep.
Write	To form words or letters on a surface as with a pen	You tell me a story, and I'll write it down.
Count	To add up with by unit so as to get a total	Count all the children in your group so we buy the right number.

Source: Dictionary definitions are from Webster's New World Compact School and Office Dictionary (1982) by Simon & Schuster.

Unit 4: SmartStart Toolbox Mediator Response Questions for the Nimble Symbol

Parent's Name: Date:

Which activities did you do?

How did they go?

What modifications would you recommend?

Did you make up any activities relevant to the Unit's goals? What were these?

How did your child react while you worked on this Unit?

Any other comments?

UNIT 5. WHAT'S THE BIG IDEA?

Rules
© C.S. Lidz
"Just follow the rules!"
I heard my friend say,
When we started to play
Our new game.
"But I don't know the rules!"
I said under my breath,
For fear I might lose
And feel shame.
Some rules can help us
To know what to do,
And others just get in our way.
I like the rules I make up myself,
Because then I know how to play.

This unit focuses on making rules, getting the main idea, and learning from generalizable principles. This unit helps children become the generators of principles derived from their experiences to offset their more typical experience in education in which they are the passive recipients of ideas formulated by others and based on the experiences of others.

A Bit of Theory

The big idea behind the Big Idea is generalization. It is primarily by understanding basic and underlying principles and overriding rules that we are able to generalize from the situation in which we learned something to another situation that shares, but does not duplicate, the original. Thinking in terms of rules and principles helps us apply learning to new situations and to become independent learners (Gallimore & Goldenberg, 1993). If we get the main idea and know the general rule, we don't have to be told what to do and how to do it each time a new situation arises or a slight change occurs.

Learning, to be effective, needs to generalize. One situation is never exactly the same as another, and if we learned only how to function or problem solve under one set of circumstances, we would never develop or progress.

Furthermore, it is simply efficient to be able to abstract and apply the basic ideas from one situation to apply to the next. Our brains would not be able to deal with having to learn every single detail of every new situation. One of the "right brain," "left brain" differences is that (in right dominant individuals) our right brain specializes in novel learning, whereas our left brain specializes in automaticity. The more we can automate, the more efficient we are. Also, the more we can generalize basic principles and rules across situations, the more efficient we are. Efficiency is important to smooth and rapid processing.

Generalization (transfer) of learned skills and knowledge is one of the most pronounced deficiencies in cognitive "profile" of internationally adopted children. Many of these children perform well below expectations for their age. This weakness has a tendency to increase in prominence if not remediated by the coordinated efforts of teachers and parents. Feuerstein et al. (1980) calls this problem "episodic grasp of reality," which accounts for the tendency of many children who develop behavior problems to fail to see the relationship between one event and another, including the relationship between their actions and the consequences of their actions.

Talk to your child about main ideas and rules; for example: "do we need a rule here?" "will it help to apply our rule?" When explaining a new game or activity to your child, try to include general principles for how to do it, and not just each step. For example, when building with blocks: "if we line up each block and don't leave any part of it sticking out, it will stay up better."

You can help your child get the main idea and summarize by doing this yourself when reading stories or when telling others of an experience that you had. Once you have modeled this for your child, encourage your child to tell others about experiences and stories. Try telling frequently read stories without reading the words. Give your child opportunities to talk with encouraging remarks such as "what do you think …", or "can you remember some more that I left out?" or "tell grandma what happened to you today!" or "tell your brother the interesting story we just read."

Generally speaking, the parents should ask more process-oriented questions that differ from content-oriented questions usually asked by the teachers during their school lessons. Some appropriate process-oriented questions would be: "Give me a reason why we should look carefully at this picture before describing it?", "Why do you think it's better to count this way?", "That's a correct answer, but can you tell me why it is correct?" Make a mistake on purpose, and ask your child if it was correct. If not, why not.

PART 1. MAIN IDEAS

Unit Objectives

- Get the main idea from listening
- Learn to appreciate, apply, and make up rules
- Abstract general principles

Activity 1: "You Tell Me Yours and I'll Tell You Mine"

The goal: To help your child summarize the main ideas of stories.
Preparation: A storybook that interests your child.

What do I say? What do I do?

1   Read a short story to your child; then have your child try to tell the story without the book; encourage your child to tell the story back to you. Try to get your child to tell just one thing, and then build up to two or three. You can also cue your child to listen for something like: "this is a story about children going to the park. Listen, and tell me what they did in the park." When your child is good at this, then try to get your child to distinguish between relatively minor details and the main events or ideas in the story. You can start this by talking about the "most important thing" in the story yourself.

2   Read stories, watch cartoons, and listen to CD recordings that teach a lesson and help your child understand the idea of the lesson, for example, of "Aesop's Fables."

Activity 2: "Headlines"

The goal: To help your child reach for the main idea of a story or an event.
Preparation: A short story or actual experience.

What do I say? What do I do?

1   Talk to your child about the way newspapers have headlines to represent the main idea of the story that follows. Give an example of something that happened to your child, such as the

first day of school, and show how there could be a headline for that: "Sarah Starts First School Day!" Practice making headlines for personal experiences (Thomas Explores New Shopping Mall; Mary Searches for Lost Dog; Mike Scrapes Knee Chasing Ball ...).

2   Look through photos of your child at an event or visit, and think up headlines to describe the picture ("Mike rides pony").

3   Cue your child to think of a headline for a bedtime story. Encourage your child to think of something different from the given title of the story, a title that includes something important that happens in the story.

4   Divide an 8 1/2 × 11" paper (or larger) in thirds or fourths and work with your child to draw sequences of a story for each section. It could be something your child makes up or something your child has read. Then, help your child come up with a headline to summarize the event in the story and write it for your child at the top or bottom of the page.

5   Make up a headline and encourage your child to make up a brief story to suit your headline, for example: "Boy Surprised by First Visit to New Park."

6   Make a family newsletter to highlight with headlines and short summaries the main events of the month. Share this with your extended family and keep it as a scrapbook reminder of your own family history.

Activity 3: "TV Gab"

The goal: To help your child summarize the main idea.
Preparation: Select a TV program appropriate for your child.

What do I say? What do I do?

1   Watch a TV story with your child and encourage your child to tell the story to someone else, for example, during playtime or during visiting. Help your child think of the main ideas of the story and to communicate these; ask your child what the most important thing was about the story. If there are disagreements about what was most important, talk about why each person thinks their idea was the most important.

You would expect the younger child just to retell some simple specific details of the story, while an older, more experienced child would be able to mix details with main ideas.

2   Help your child compose a letter to a TV station to evaluate their programming. Pick either a station with favorite shows or one that concerns you and your child.

PART 2. PRINCIPLES AND RULES

Activity 1: "Rules for My Space"

The goal: To help your child understand that we can use rules to guide our behavior.
Preparation: No preparation.

What do I say? What do I do?

1   Talk to your child about the rules we have for different things, such as how to behave at home, or how to act when you ride a bus or eat. For the younger children, introduce ideas about rules for behavior just before they need to be applied ("hold my hand when you cross the street") and while "correcting" your child for a misdemeanor (for example, "when we visit someone, we don't open their drawers.")

2   Talk about how rules can help us and the reason for the rule. For example, we need rules for traffic, or it would be easy for people to get hurt. For older children, you might also want to discuss how there can sometimes be bad rules or too many rules, but you first want to make the point that rules can help to keep the world orderly and safe.

3   Jointly, make up some rules for the family and house that will help to make life easier; some of these can be arrived at democratically, while others may need a more directive approach "because I'm the Mom or Dad."

4   Suggest thinking up some rules for what your child values at home, such as the bedroom or toys. Write out the rules your child makes up and give others at home a chance to make up their rules. Talk about which ones are easy to

follow, while others may cause some problems, and some compromises might be necessary. After several days, review the rules to see how well they worked or if any changes need to be made. Talk about why it was an easy or good rule or why it may not have been a good rule. This is a good time to use symbols.

Activity 2: "The Rules of the Game"

The goal: To help your child understand the need to follow rules to play games.

Preparation: A game with rules, such as Candy Land, or Simon Says, Red Light/Green Light.

What do I say? What do I do?

1   Suggest playing any familiar game with your child, but before you begin, ask your child to remind you about the rules of the game that you have "forgotten."

2   Talk about how to play the game in terms of "what are the rules for this game?" Monitor the playing in terms of how well the rules are being followed and how it stops being fun for the others when one person decides to break the rules. Young children can play simple ball and other kinds of movement games, while older children can move onto board games.

Activity 3: "It's the Principle of the Thing"

The goal: To help your child understand the basic principles underlying their activities and games.

Preparation: A construction toy such as blocks, legos, or tinkertoy.

What do I say? What do I do?

1   While constructing a tower or a building that involves balance, discuss general principles such as the need to use a

wide base for a tall tower and equal weight for balance. In working with your child on any construction toy, wait until your child experiences some difficulty, and offer a suggestion that recognizes the basic principle of construction, rather than telling your child too specifically to "put that one here" or "that one there." Talk more in terms of "if .... then ..." that allows your child to use the idea in other situations. The complexity of the construct and the level of your discussion would vary with the age of your child. Let your child first show you the type of construction he or she can do, and then offer your comments to suit the needs of the situation.

Table 3.5 Vocabulary list for Unit 5: What's the Big Idea?

The words you use	What the dictionary says	What you might say
Principle	A fundamental truth, law upon which others are based	I want you to understand the basic principle. That's not the point! It's the principle that counts!
Rule	A guide for conduct	Let me read the rules of the game before we play. I think we need a rule here; we're getting confused.
Precise	Accurately stated; Exact	That was really a very precise description. He's a very precise person.
Clue	A fact or object that helps to solve a mystery or a problem	Give me a clue, and then maybe I can figure it out. I don't have a clue about what you mean.

Source: Dictionary definitions are from Webster's New World Compact School and Office Dictionary (1982) by Simon & Schuster.

Unit 5: SmartStart Toolbox Mediator Response Questions for What's the Big Idea

Parent's Name: Date

Which activities did you do?

How did they go?

What modifications would you recommend?

Did you make up any activities relevant to the Unit's goals? What were these?

How did your child react while you worked on this Unit?

Any other comments?

UNIT 6. SELF-REGULATION/SELF-CONTROL

Who's in charge?
© C.S. Lidz
I run when I walk.
I slur when I talk.
I don't know why,
I just spec-u-late.
When my mom's on the phone,
I can't leave her alone.
She gets mad and says that
I agg-ra-vate.
I can't seem to wait
To get more on my plate.
I want it right now!
So I ag-i-tate.
My feelings are strong.
I cry when I'm wrong'd.
It sometimes is true
I exag-er-ate.
My fast is too fast.
My slow is too slow.
It's so hard for me.
To self-regulate!

This unit focuses on development of self-regulation. Children need to learn to control themselves and to reduce their dependence upon control by others. Self-regulation is something that develops in spurts throughout your child's growth, from early childhood through adolescence; however, it is beginning to emerge during the preschool years.

A Bit of Theory

The attention of both researchers and practitioners has turned increasingly to the issue of development of self-regulation in children. The capacity for self-regulation is inherent in our nervous system, and specifically the work of our late-developing prefrontal lobe. This represents an executive capacity that involves not only inhibition of impulsivity, but also allocation of resources and appropriate timing of responses to enable us to develop and reach our goals and, at the same time, get along with others.

The process for developing this internalization was elaborated by Vygotsky and those influenced by his work, such as Luria. Vygotsky noted the development of self-regulation first through the external sources (efforts of others, parents first of all), moving to explicit self-talk, further moving to internalized private self-talk, and then total internalization. The primary tool for enabling this process was viewed as language: the parents talk the child through experiences; the child then learns to talk to himself or herself through experiences and problem solution following the model of the caregiver, and the child then moves to independent thinking and self-regulation. Such opportunities for optimal mediation, according to Feuerstein's and Vygotsky's theories, promote higher mental processes that include the ability to self-regulate.

It is important to realize that, whereas the capacity for self-regulation is inherent in the organism, the skills for self-regulation need to be learned and can be taught (Bradley & Caldwell, 1984). Children will of course have their individual differences, but there is considerable plasticity that can respond to experience in most children. Children develop self-regulation most successfully from what has been termed an "authoritative" rather than an "authoritarian" parent. The authoritative leader helps children learn to think for themselves by encouraging, facilitating, modeling independent thinking, and providing consultation and information as needed. The authoritarian leader, on the other hand, dictates, orders, and expects unquestioning compliance; such experiences may produce order so long as the leader is present to enforce rewards and punishments, which usually dissipates without this presence.

Post-institutionalized children come from an environment where they lived in a highly controlled authoritarian setting: meals, study and play time, even hygiene routines were all done in groups and on a fixed schedule. One of the characteristics of overseas orphanages is a peculiar combination of rigid routine with ongoing uncontrollable (by the children) changes in the environment. The frequent turnover of caregivers leads to a tremendous sense of instability and lack of control. On the other hand, children's everyday routines are fixed; there are virtually no personal choices and very few private possessions of toys or other goods. Self-regulation of behavior and emotions is not facilitated under such conditions; indeed, there is a minimal need for behavioral self-regulation.

Institutions are not capable of being consistently responsive to the individual differences of the particular child. The child learns to be an object of discipline. Some of these children internalize this model to such an extent that they simply transfer to their post-institutionalized lives strategies that used to be effective in their previous lives. Special and well thought out actions and teaching strategies are needed to teach post-institutionalized children self-discipline and self-regulation that will help them adapt to their new circumstances.

Immaturity in self-regulation of behavior and emotions reveals itself in such behavior patterns as:

- Difficulty following rules governing behavior: although children may be well aware of a rule and able to explain it to you, they are unable to control their impulsive actions.
- Reluctance or total unwillingness to do tasks which are repetitive, uninteresting, which require effort, and which have not been chosen by the child (but that is what life in general and much of school learning in particular consist of!).
- Emotional volatility. These children are easily aroused emotionally: whether happy or sad, the speed and intensity with which they move to the extreme of their emotions is much greater than that of their same age peers; they are often on a roller coaster ride of emotions. As observed by one parent: "When my 8-year-old is happy, he is so happy that people tell him to calm down. When he is unhappy, he is so unhappy that people tell him to calm down."
- Difficulty with delaying gratification and accepting "No" for an answer. In this respect many post-institutionalized children are more similar to much younger children than to peers.

On arrival into the family, this arrangement is drastically changed: the old structured setting is eliminated and an adjustment to a new order is on the immediate agenda. In addition, due to language-related problems, even minimal control of a situation by a child may become a rather complex and stressful task. No wonder that practically all internationally adopted children initially demonstrate lack of self-regulation skills and are at a high risk for many problems – from persistent tantrums, to impulsive behaviors, to difficulty with sleeping and eating. When a child develops these missing self-regulation skills, he or she will feel more comfortable and act more mature when faced with the inevitable emotional, social, and cognitive challenges at home and at school.

In order to develop self-regulation skills, children need to be involved in activities where self-regulation is practiced. Adoptive parents play an important role by helping children learn to use talk to solve problems and to think flexibly about different ways to overcome obstacles and to make things happen. Children also learn to regulate themselves by regulating others, that is, by engaging in activities such as playing teacher, father, mother. This unit relates to all of the others, but mostly to "Let's Make a Plan." We need to control our impulses in order to make plans and build toward a future. The answer to "who's in charge" is "first you; then me."

Unit Objectives

- Learn to regulate movements
- Learn to regulate attention
- Learn to regulate feelings

Part 1. Main Ideas

Activity 1: "Relax"

The goal: To promote your child's self-awareness and ability to control her or his body.

Preparation: As a supplement to a quiet-down activity just prior to bedtime, while your child is reclining in bed, try a relaxation exercise regime such as this. Once your child has gained some experience with this, you can refer to it at times during the day when your child appears particularly tense or wound up.

What do I say? What do I do?

1   Tell your child:

Let's try a new game tonight. We'll do this together. This is called the "relaxation game." I'm going to tell you to close your eyes. Then we will make different parts of our body real tight and tense. Then we'll make the same part of our body very loose and relaxed. Let's try it. First, I'll name the part of the body, then next time, we can take turns telling the names.

Use a soft somewhat monotone voice, speaking slowly with pauses. If your child has difficulty controlling the specific part of the body named, touch that area lightly while your child tries to tense or relax it.

"OK. Now close your eyes. Make your eyes close really tight. Crunch your eyelids together. OK. Now relax your eyes.

Make your eyes really loose and relaxed. Good. Now make your mouth really tight, like you are very mad. Good. Now, relax your mouth, really loose and relaxed."

Continue to identify body parts, focusing on those that your child can most easily control, such as hands, toes, shoulders, stomach.

Activity 2: "Mirror, Mirror!"

The goal: To promote body control through imitating the movements of a partner.

Preparation: Identify a partner who would be acceptable and fun for your child, including yourself, or a sibling, or a friend.

What do I say? What do I do?

1 Tell your child: "Here's a new fun game I call the Mirror Game! Each person has a partner. Then, with your partner, each person takes turn being the mirror and the copier." Use whatever names you wish to communicate the ideas. "First, the mirror makes a move [demonstrate], and the copier has to do exactly the same move as the mirror. Let's try some!" Start with some simple moves that are easy to copy, then get as difficult and silly as you wish to suit the age and personality of your child. Do about five moves before changing roles.

Activity 3: "Red Light"

The goal: This is an old, traditional game that promotes body control in response to a visual cue.

Preparation: Prepare a sheet of paper with a large red circle in the middle. This is the most fun with a group, but can be played with just two people.

What do I say? What do I do?

1 Tell your child: "Here's a fun game for you. It's called: "Red light." Just like the light we see for cars out on the street. You know how red means stop, and green means go?

Well, this red circle means stop. One of us will be the police person who is in charge of the light. The others have to do what the light says. The police person stands here (in front), with back turned. You all stand very far away. Your job is to try to sneak up on the police person and tag him/her. The one who is the first to tag the police person gets to do that job next. BUT, you have to stop when the light says stop. AND, you may not run." Demonstrate the role of police for your child. Turn your back, holding the red light, and quickly turn around to show it. Coach your child to sneak up quietly when your back is turned to try to tag you, and to stop when you turn around to show the light. Once the child learns this game, the rules can be made more stringent so that the child must stop and show no body movement when the red light appears. Any movement means they are out of the game.

Activity 4: "First Say; then Do"

The goal: To teach impulse control by interjecting words before actions, and to control movements by directed, intentional action.

Preparation: A ball of any size that your child can roll, and nonbreakable toys that can serve as targets. The larger the ball, the greater the chance that your child can hit the target. Place them at a distance that maximizes your child's chances of being able to hit them with the rolling ball.

What do I say? What do I do?

Tell your child: "This is a special kind of ball game. We're going to sit on the floor and roll this ball. We'll try to hit one of those toys with the ball. BUT, first, you have to say which toy you are going to touch. THEN you roll the ball and try to hit it. Watch me do it first." Please note that you have to use a whole sentence such as: "Now I'm going to hit the toy bear."

Activity 5: "Listen up!"

The goal: To help your child focus attention and coordinate actions with listening.

Preparation: A familiar storybook or favorite poem.

What do I say? What do I do?

Ask your child to listen for a word or a sound in a poem or story and clap every time this occurs. Select a word or sound that recurs. Substitute any action or sound for clapping; the important idea is to get your child to listen and to indicate when the target has been noticed. You can use the same story or poem for multiple target words or sounds; in fact, this is recommended, as it will help your child develop even more control, since your child would need to shift attention.

Activity 6: "All the World's a Stage"

The goal: You and your child act out different feelings from a short story.

Preparation: A storybook with lots of action and expression of feelings.

What do I say? What do I do?

Read the story to your child with the idea of listening for different feelings and reactions of the characters. If the feeling is stated in the story, ask your child to act this out (model this if necessary). If the feeling is not stated, ask your child to say how the character might be feeling, and then act this out.

Activity 7: "When You're Happy and You Know It …"

The goal: To provide an opportunity to talk about emotions and how they are expressed.

Preparation: Paper and drawing implements (crayons or markers).

What do I say? What do I do?

Draw pictures together to help talk about different feelings. "Let's draw a happy picture." Ask your child: "What are things that make you feel happy/sad/angry/scared. What's an OK way to express negative feelings, especially anger?"

Activity 8: "Taking Turns as Boss"

The goal: To give your child an opportunity to give you instructions, that is, to tell you what to do.

Preparation: Prepare a short deck of cards (such as index cards) with simple drawings on each that show actions (e.g., stand up, stick out your tongue, scratch your head, kick your foot, scratch someone's back, say something nice about the other person, and so on).

Tell your child: "We're going to play a fun card game. We each get a turn to tell each other (or the next person) what to do." Review the cards with your child to ensure that the actions can be understood; then mix them up again. Take turns selecting a card, and say the sentence: "I want you to … (do the activity on the card)."

Table 3.6 Vocabulary list for Unit 6: Who Is in Charge?

The words you use	What the dictionary says	What you might say
Self-control	Control of one's emotions, desires, actions	Let's work on developing some self-control. He sure doesn't have any self-control. Wow, you sure showed good self-control.
Self-regulate	Same as self-control	Let's get that self-regulation in gear. Self-regulation is really important for this.
Attention	Mental concentration or readiness	Are you paying attention? First, I need your attention.

Source: Dictionary definitions are from Webster's New World Compact School and Office Dictionary (1982) by Simon & Schuster.

Unit 6: SmartStart Toolbox Mediator Response Questions for Who Is in Charge?

Parent's Name: Date:

Which activities did you do?

How did they go?

What modifications would you recommend?

Did you make up any activities relevant to the Unit's goals? What were these?

How did your child react while you worked on this Unit?

Any other comments?

UNIT 7. MAKING CONNECTIONS TO STRENGTHEN ATTACHMENT

Family
© C. S. Lidz
My home is such a busy place,
With people in and out.
I sometimes like my time alone
When I can think about
All the funny things that families can be,
Some good, some bad, some happy, sad,
And how it feels to be like me.

A Bit of Theory

As described in the *Introduction* to this program, attachment provides the foundation for healthy, intimate relationships in adoptive families. This unit is devoted to a very important aspect of adoptive family life: connections between past, present, and future in the context of your family. It is done through the range of attachment-building opportunities, using playful activities that are interactive, include body contact, do not require special equipment, can take place anywhere/anytime, promote security and trust, and encourage feelings of belonging and being valued.

In general, there are several aspects in this theme for which adoptive parents and in particular school teachers need to be sensitive and tactful. First, the adopted children usually do not have photos or any other evidence of early childhood (that normally exist in biologically started families), except for their court decrees and medical papers. It can be traumatic for adopted children in school when they are required to do something like "My Family Tree" assignments or are asked to bring their pictures as babies. That is why, such assignments as: "special things that happened to me, my favorite thing to say, something I did for the first time, how I celebrated my birthday, places I went to see" in relation to a pre-adoptive era will not be possible for children adopted before the age of four and possibly traumatic for those who were adopted after this age.

Another important aspect of making connections between past and present that also needs to be reinforced is that, when talking with your child, try to refer to things that you did together in your shared past that relate to what you are doing now. Use words like: "remember when …?"; "this reminds me of …"; or, "when was another time we …?" You are building a "new" past, so this accumulating history can be used to make time and space connections.

Unit Objectives

• Build and strengthen attachment through playful activities.
• Become aware of interrelationships within families

We want to reinforce the importance of fun and playfulness as an effective ingredient of learning: there is a need for children to develop emotionally and socially, as well as cognitively. If development of higher levels of thinking takes place within relationships, it is best for these relationships to be positive, supportive, and enjoyable. Connecting learning with emotion is an effective tool for memory.

Activity 1: "Let's Play Together"

The goal: To promote attachment though playful activities.
Preparation: None.

What do I say? What do I do?

For children ages 4–5:

"Giant Walk": The child stands on your feet, facing you, walk them around the room. Your rule: eye contact makes you go while lack of eye contact makes you stop.

"Eye Blinking Contest" game: Stare at each other and see who can go the longest without blinking or laughing. Winner gives the looser a hug or tickle.

"Brooklyn Bridge" game: Both parents start by kneeling on the floor to form a tunnel and tell the child that it looks like a bridge that will collapse soon, so he/she needs to pass under the bridge as fast as possible. During the first few times, let the child get completely through, then have "the bridge" gently collapse onto your child with laughs and hugs.

"Guess What is in the Mouth" game: Ask your child to close her/his eyes and put in his/her mouth a small treat (a piece of carrot, cheese, berry, etc.) and ask what it was.

"Pillow ride" game: Have child sit on a big floor pillow and drag him/her around the room. Your rule: you only move when given eye contact.

For children ages 6–8

"Remember Me" game: Ask your child to look at you attentively because you are going to change your appearance soon. Then leave the room and return after you've changed something in your appearance. Ask your child what is different about you now. For the younger children it could be something rather obvious (for example, you put a hat on your head and changed the jacket). For older children it could be unbutton a button or taken off earrings.

"Copycat" game: The idea is to have the parent playfully copy what the child is doing (such as clapping his/her hands). Eye contact, smiles, and laughs are part of the game. Mirroring can also be done as in the above unit.

Thumb wrestling: Hold each other's forearms, and sit facing and touching each other with your knees. Pretend you are applying great effort to hold your arms straight. Another version is to interlock either your right or left hands with your thumbs free and on top. The thumbs "fight" to try to hold down the one of the "opponent." Helping your child to self-regulate may become an issue here, but a good time to work on it.

Activity 2: "We're Connected"

The goal: To help your child become aware of her or his relationship with the various members of your family and their relationships with each other.

Preparation: Photographs of the members of your family and a place to paste them.

What do I say? What do I do?

1   Collect photographs of the most familiar members of your family. Review these with your child and try to help your child recognize them by telling something special about them, including their relationship to your child. You might have photos of some members at different ages in their lives; show these to your child and talk about the ages and where

they were at the time. Make your child feel an inseparable part of the family, where he or she has a relationship history and ties with the other members. Remember, for most adopted children the experience of belonging to a family is totally new. Make the emphasis that they are now a part of the "clan," that they "belong," that their history from now on is intertwined with the "histories" of other members of the family.

2 Look at photos of extended members of your family, and place those who are related close to each other. Explain to your child how they are related to each other and to you and your child. Make an album that shows the groupings within your family. When a family member visits, use this as a reference sheet to rehearse names and personal details.

3 Do a family interview of one of the older members of your family. Decide with your child what it might be interesting to know. Get the answers to your questions, and ask that family member to show photographs and tell some family stories. If you have the equipment, make a video or audio recording of the interview.

4 When someone from the family comes to visit (or you visit them), ask your child to ask them to tell something they remember when they were your child's age.

Activity 3: "Adoption LifeBook"

Many adoptive parents have what is called "Adoption LifeBook," where they collect information about their adopted children. The purpose of the LifeBook is to connect related life events and gain perspective on life's past events. The very creation of the LifeBook is a productive share/joint activity for all family members to facilitate attachment. This activity can be especially valuable, but also equally painful: coming to understand one's past is the way to prepare for the future. You can read more about Adoption LifeBook "technology" in Beth O'Malley's website at: Beth O'Malley's Adoption Lifebooks | Articles by Adult Adoptee – Lifebooks are Magic.

Activity 4: "Finding the Source"

The goal: To help your child understand where common objects in
  the environment come from.
Preparation: Depending upon level, you need a place to visit, or a
  book to read.

What do I say? What do I do?

1   If you ask most children (at least those in the city) where
    something comes from, they will usually say "the store."
    Think about what is available in your community that you
    can visit to show your child where something is made. Is there
    a place where cars, ice cream, money, clothes, toys, candy, etc.
    are made? Many of these places offer tours.
2   Find a book in the library that talks about where the food
    we eat comes from. Take your child to the supermarket and
    remind your child of what the book said: "do you remember
    where eggs come from? Milk? Bacon? etc."
3   Visit a place where things are made, and, after you return
    home, encourage your child to recall the sequence of the
    manufacture, and draw a picture to show the progression.
    See if you can find a place that sells the exact thing you
    saw made.
4   Look for books that describe how things are made and
    where they come from. Help make your child aware of other
    parts of the country and the world that have raw materials
    for things that you use; read about these places and, if the
    child can relate to a map, show your child where these places
    are. Read labels when you buy clothes for your children and
    tell them where the clothes are made; see if you can find it
    on a map.

Part 2. Family Relationships

Activity 1: "Ritually Speaking"

The goal: To build a memory for your child of something that was
  special, constant, and predictable for your family.
Preparation: No preparation.

What do I say? What do I do?

1 Try to think of something that you could do within your family as a "ritual" that you could repeat perhaps weekly or monthly. This could be something like reading a story together as a family after dinner once each week, or having an "outing night" once a week, or bringing in a video, or taking turns at the table each sharing something important that happened that week, or "performance night," where every family member would select something to present – a story to read, a poem, a song to sing, etc. The idea is that it is repeatable, special to your family and your child knows that "it's Wednesday, it must be ..." It should be something that most family members enjoy. Invite a friend or relative to share in the ritual.

2 Establish some new rituals/celebrations related to your child. It can be on the day your child arrived in America, the day of adoption, etc. It could be a celebration similar to a birthday, or a trip to some special place.

3 Help your child learn about cultural rituals within your family, as well as from other cultures; talk about which ones you follow and which you do not.

Activity 2: "Let Them Read History"

The goal is to increase your internationally adopted child's awareness of their own cultural background and make the child understand that it is OK to be different, and it's OK to come to America from some other place. In the initial stages of your child's life in America your son or daughter may desperately want to be like the other kids: dress the same, speak the same language, have the same toys, have an American name. At those stages it may be detrimental and painful to a child to remind him or her about being different and standing out of a crowd. So, when you talk about the roots and the virtues of being different, let the child gradually come to this conclusion based on other people's experiences and past; do not accentuate the child's differences: give the examples of being different, coming from the other country and being proud of that, based on your own life, or on the life of those who your child admires. Be very careful with the references to your child's pre-adoption experiences and cultural artifacts that may very well be unwanted reminders despite of your best intensions and expectations.

Table 3.7 Vocabulary list for Unit 7: Making Connections to Strengthen Attachment

The words you use	What the dictionary says	What you might say
Relationship	Connection between person or things	What's the relationship between these? I don't see any relationship.
Cause	Anything producing an effect or result; A reason or motive for some action	What could have caused that?
Effect	Anything brought about by a cause; Result; The power to cause results	This really makes an interesting effect. If I do it this way, what effect will it have?
Past	A former time; time gone by; The history of a person or group	Do you remember what we did for your past birthday? In the past, we used to do it like this.
Present	Existing or happening now	For the present, let's try it this way. We can't just think about the present; we need to plan for the future.
Family	Parents and their children; All those descended from a common ancestor	We have a very close family.
Change	To make different; Substitute, alter	We're going out; you need to change your clothes. Look how it changes when you do that.
Culture	The skills, arts, etc. of a given period; Civilization	This is a song that is characteristic of our culture.

Source: Dictionary definitions are from Webster's New World Compact School and Office Dictionary (1982) by Simon & Schuster.

Unit 7: SmartStart Toolbox Mediator Response Questions for Making Connections to Strengthen Attachment

Parent's Name: Date:

Which activities did you do?

How did they go?

What modifications would you recommend?

Did you make up any activities relevant to the Unit's goals? What were these?

How did your child react while you worked on this Unit?

Any other comments?

SmartStart Toolbox: Workshop Program Evaluation

Please give us your feedback about your experience as a participant in this program.

You may provide your name, or do this anonymously.

Your Name: _____
Program Leader: _____
Dates of Workshop: _____

What is your overall rating of this Program?

Great/ Loved It	Good	OK	Could have been better	Poor
5	4	3	2	1

What did you like best?

What could have been better?

What were your goals when you took the program?

To what extent did you meet your goals?

Totally	Mostly	Some	Few	None
5	4	3	2	1

Would you recommend this to a friend?

Yes; definitely	Probably	Maybe	No
4	3	2	1

Do you feel you can go on to incorporate the principles and ideas of this Program in your ongoing interactions with your child?

Yes, for sure	Probably	Perhaps	No
4	3	2	1

What would you like us to know that we haven't asked?

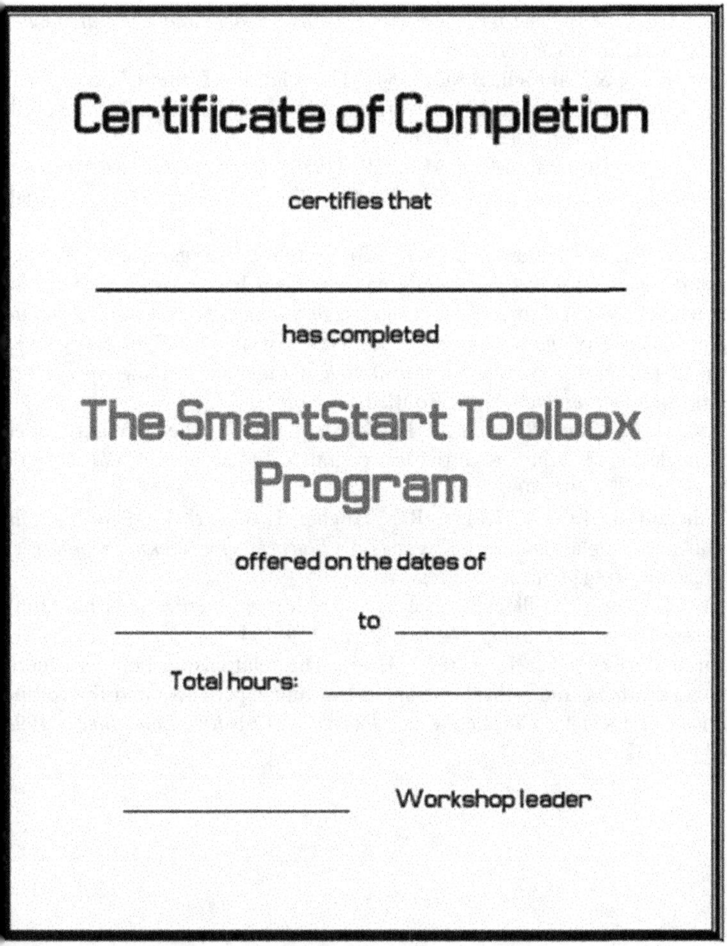

Certificate of Completion

certifies that

_____

has completed

The SmartStart Toolbox Program

offered on the dates of

_____   to   _____

Total hours: _____

_____   Workshop leader

Figure 3.1 A blank Certificate of Completion.

References

Agnes, M.E. (1982). *Webster's new world compact school and office dictionary.* New York: Simon & Schuster.

Bradley, R.H., & Caldwell, B.M. (1984). The relation of infants' home environments to achievement test performance in first grade: A follow-up study. *Child Development, 55*(3), 803–809.

Feuerstein, R., Hoffman, M., & Miller, R. (1980). *Instrumental enrichment: An intervention program for cognitive modifiability.* Baltimore, MD: University Park Press.

Gallimore, R., & Goldenberg, C. (1993). Activity settings in early literacy. Home and school factors in children's emergent literacy. In E.A. Forman, N. Minick, & C.A. Stone (Eds.). *Contexts for literacy: Sociocultural dynamics in children's development* (pp. 315–335). New York: Oxford University Press.

Gindis, B. (2019) *Child development mediated by trauma: The dark side of international adoption.* New York: Routledge.

Mackner, L.M., Starr, R.H., Jr., & Black, M.M. (1997). The cumulative effect of neglect and failure to thrive on cognitive functioning. *Child Abuse & Neglect, 21*(7), 691–700.

McGillicuddy-DeLisi, A., DeLisi, R., Flaugher, J., & Sigel, I. (1986). Familial influences on planning. In J. Kagan (Ed.) *Blueprints for thinking. Cambridge,* UK: Cambridge University Press.

Rutter, M. (1999). Resilience concepts and findings: Implications for family therapy. *Journal of Family Therapy, 21*(2), 119–144.

Zambrana-Ortiz, N., & Lidz, C.S. (1995). The relationship between Puerto Rican mothers' and fathers' mediated learning experiences and the competencies of their preschool children. *Journal of Cognitive Education in 1995, 4*(1), 17–32.

4 The SmartStart Toolbox Program as a Basis for Diagnosis and Prescription

This chapter offers an opportunity for professionals who work with parents to use the SmartStart Toolbox Program as a diagnostic assessment within the Dynamic Assessment framework. The chapter includes profiles for recording the pre and post program interactions of mediators, as well as the responsiveness of their children to this mediation. Within the pretest-intervene-posttest format of dynamic assessment, the activities within the units of Chapter 3 offer the selection of interventions for this process. The chapter ends with a chart to facilitate match-making between the needs of the child and the interventions offered by the mediator.

The SmartStart Toolbox Program was designed to deliver an optimal Mediated Learning Experience (MLE) to young international adoptees. In essence, the Toolbox offers predesigned activities that are used in a relatively standardized way by the parents enrolled in the SmartStart workshops. However, it is also possible to use the same program as a diagnostic-prescriptive process that can target and address specific needs of both children and parents as they navigate their experiences. This chapter describes a model for using the SmartStart as a diagnostic/ prescriptive tool. In this chapter we discuss the use of the program by professionals such as psychologists or social workers, who are trained and certified within their professions, to provide clinical services. We assume that these professionals are knowledgeable and experienced in conducting assessments and interventions. In order to convert the Toolbox into a diagnostic-prescriptive instrument, the professionals will need to add the assessment component suggested in this chapter. This application of the SmartStart Toolbox Program then becomes a Curriculum-based Dynamic Assessment, as described by Lidz (2003).

The dynamic assessment model used here proceeds in a test-intervene-retest format. For our purposes, the child's ability to perform

DOI: 10.4324/9781003253587-5

the selected activity becomes both pretest and retest, and mediated interactions involving the same activity become the intervention. The model can be applied in at least two ways, first, to the assessor's engagement with the child, and second, to observations of the parent's interactions with the child. For example, in the case of the assessor's interaction with the child, suppose the activity of leaf collection during a nature walk is selected as the activity.

The "pretest" for this would simply be something like: "Let's take a walk and make a collection of some leaves. It's the fall, and all kinds of leaves are on the ground. You decide which ones you would like to collect, and I'll do it also." Proceed to walk and collect. [pretest] "Great. Let's see what we have. I decided to pick up the ones with lots of points; they shouldn't be broken, and they should have at least two colors. Let's see what you collected." [Review child's collection to see if there is any recurring pattern or point of reference for the collection. Discuss both collections with the child focusing on details and patterns to notice. [intervention]. "Great. Now let's make another collection. What will you notice this time?" Review the collections with the child and talk about what changed. Make note if the child's basis for the collection has changed, and in what way. What you are looking for is the child's ability to change and improvement in the child's ability to notice details and use these as a basis for the collection. Some children may even go on to use the details as the basis for making a pattern or for creative extensions such as clothing for dolls. When applied to observations of the parent's interactions, the separation of phases would be done in the processing of the observer, and the focus of the assessment would be on the parent as mediator.

The child's first interactions with the materials would serve as "pretest"; the ongoing interactions of the parent or professional with the child during the course of the activity would be the "intervention," and the child's responsiveness to these interactions would comprise the "retest." Alternatively, for those who wish to make this a more formal procedure, the parents can be coached to be more active in their interactions for the purpose of inducing changes with a more formal pretest and retest where the parent simply presents the material and lets the child proceed without interaction. In this model, we are not concerned with scores, but with noticing the details and qualities of the interactions and their effects on the child. We are also interested in the response of the parents to these effects. All aspects of the interactions are open for transparent discussion with both the parent and the child as they work together to create the most enjoyable and effective learning experience for the child.

To actually carry out the details of this model, the *Mediated Learning Experience Rating Scale* (MLERS; Lidz, 2003, pp. 74–75) and *Response to Mediation Scale* (RMS; Lidz, 2003, pp. 124–126) should be used. Both of these scales are discussed here in terms of the information they provide to the assessment process. This chapter contains the analysis of the processes involved in the SmartStart Toolbox Units, which enables the assessor to make a prescriptive match with the activities in the units that meet the needs of the child in the most efficient way. The two abovementioned scales are used for helping clinicians establish the needs of the children, and enable their parents to offer the child the most appropriate interventions within *The SmartStart Toolbox Program.*

Mediated Learning Experience (MLE)

In Chapter 2 we presented basic tenets of the concept of MLE as created by Reuven Feuerstein and his colleagues (Feuerstein, Hoffman, Rand, & Miller, 1980). Based on this theoretical foundation, Lidz (1991, 2003) has developed the MLERS. The MLERS operationalizes the major components of the MLE approach (see Chapter 2) into observable behaviors that are rated by a professional clinician or researcher while watching the parent (mediator) interact with the child during the course of a shared activity. The Scale provides a profile of the mediator's current mediational repertory.

The SmartStart Toolbox Program embeds the components of MLE within each unit. These usually appear in the introductory comments, as well as within the instructions for the activities. What is different about the model presented here is that the MLE components are made explicit, and rated to determine the parent's current repertory of mediation skills and needs for intervention so that their interactions can be optimized to enable them to enhance their child's mental development.

To describe the parent as a mediator and apply the MLERS, it is necessary to observe the parent in interaction with the child while engaged in more than one activity. The parent's behaviors are rated for each of the activities and then averaged to create a profile (see below). (Also note that a profile can be created for each activity if the clinician wishes to evaluate the effects of the situation on the parent's mediation).

The following list is provided to give the reader an idea of how the MLE components are represented in the parent version of the MLERS.

What follows is a scale that was designed to help parents understand these components. This Scale has been used as a handout for parents in workshops to enable them to evaluate their progress in the program. It is offered here to give the reader a simple definition of each component.

The 12 types of interactions presented below are components of MLE and include direct instructions on what to tell the child ("implied message to the child") and what to do during the activity. This can be used as a checklist for parents to evaluate their own (preferably videotaped) interactions.

- **Intentionality** addresses the child's process of attention; it represents the mediator's ability to engage the child in the interaction and maintain the child's participation. The mediator expresses the intent to involve the child in a shared activity.
  Implied message to the child: *"This is what I want you to do; let me help you pay attention so you can do this."*
  To do: communicate clearly what you want and work to maintain the attention of your child.
- **Meaning** addresses the child's process of perception. The mediator helps the child notice the important things to notice about the materials involved in the interaction, including their distinguishing features and importance to enjoying/solving the activity.
  Implied message: *"Let me help you notice and learn what is important and valuable to know about what we are doing together."*
  To do: Let your child know what is important to notice by your tone of voice and what you say. Give your child elaborated information about the specific features of the materials and activities you are doing together.
- **Bridging** helps the child to form a conceptual bridge between what can be seen/heard/felt in the present situation and its relationship with what cannot be tangibly experienced, but only mentally conceptualized either in the future or from the past.
  Implied message: *"This experience is not only meaningful now, but it relates to other things we have done before or that you will do in the future."*
  To do: Relate what you are doing together to something the child knows about or has done before to something that will happen in the future; help your child apply cause/effect or what-if/then ideas.
- **Joint Regard** refers to the feeling of "togetherness" about the interaction; 'we are learning about this together." More importantly, it

also refers to the empathic understanding generated by the mediator and the ability of the mediator to "read" the child's thoughts and feelings even if not well expressed.

Implied message: *"We are having a learning experience together and I understand you as a learner."*

To do: Look at and comment on what has caught your child's attention and make statements that show that you understand how your child is feeling and thinking.

- **Sharing** calls for the mediator's sharing his or her own thinking and experiences, related to the interaction in a way that enhances the child's current experiences. It relates to Bridging since it concerns a reference that is not tangible within the situation but can only be envisioned. Care needs to be taken to avoid being intrusive into the child's learning experience.

Implied message: *"Let me tell you about some of my thoughts and experiences that relate to what we are doing together."*

To do: Share your thoughts and experiences that relate to the activity you are doing together and briefly tell your child about something you remember in your life that relates to what you are doing together.

- **Task Regulation** describes the actual task manipulations, including instructions, that address the child's capacity to perform that lead to the development of competence with it.
- **Implied message:** *"You are competent and able to learn this. I will find a way to help you learn."*
- **To do:** Give clear and simple directions; make adjustments to the materials that will help your children succeed; tell or show some general problem-solving principle that can be applied to this and other similar situations; communicate the idea of proceeding according to a plan and applying a strategy. Help the child determine if a strategy is needed, if so, did it work; if not, how it can be improved.
- **Praise and Encouragement** offer verbal or nonverbal encouragement and complimentary remarks to help motivate the child's engagement; develop a positive relationship with the child, and provide feedback about what worked. This attaches an emotional component to the task and aids in transfer to other similar situations.
- **Implied message:** *"I appreciate you and am confident that you can learn."*
- **To do**: Praise your child by words or gestures and describe what was so good, or needs more work (and what kind).
- **Psychological Differentiation** maintains the focus of the engagement on the learner, removing intrusion of the mediator into the

child's development of competence. It is helpful to think about "Who's task is this?"

Implied message: *"I am here to help you have a successful learning experience, not for my own experience."*

To do: Maintain the role of helper and mediator and avoid intrusions into learning.

- **Challenge** is the major opportunity for the mediator to create a zone of proximal development that asks the child to reach beyond his/her current level of functioning without experiencing frustration.

  Implied message: *"I want you to reach beyond what you already know or can do. Stretch yourself. I will help you by keeping the task just ahead, but not too far beyond what you can do by yourself."*

  To do: Keep the task within your children's "challenge zone," not too easy and not too hard, and avoid frustrating your child.

- **Change** documents that the child has in fact advanced as the result of an interaction. This can either be a verbal description of the child's improvement or actual documentation of the outcome of the interaction.

  Implied message: *"You can learn. Here is evidence of your ability to learn."*

  To do: Provide concrete evidence of changes your child has made as a result of your work together; help your child notice what has changed.

- **Contingent Responsiveness** creates an ongoing context of the mediator responding to the child's behavior in a timely and appropriate way.

  Implied message: *"I will notice and respond promptly and appropriately to your cues and signals to help you have a good learning experience."*

  To do: Notice and read your child's cues and respond promptly and appropriately to these signals.

- **Affective Warmth** refers to the provision of a context of warmth and joy in the interaction.

  Implied message: *"I love you, care about you, and want you to have a good experience."*

  To do: Communicate feelings of joy and affection verbally and nonverbally.

To parents: please review each of the components above and place a checkmark on the form below to indicate the level you feel you have accomplished. Then review these results with your consultant.

MLE Checklist for Parents

Interaction	Accomplished	Pretty Good	Developing	Needs Work
Intentionality				
Meaning				
Bridging				
Joint Regard				
Sharing				
Task Regulation				
Praise and Encouragement				
Psychological Differentiation				
Challenge				
Change				
Contingent Responsiveness				
Affective Warmth				

In the context of the diagnostic/prescriptive model presented here, the consultant would generate a profile of the parent-as-mediator based on administration of the MLERS (Lidz, 2003), using Table below. This form serves to document the strengths and needs of the parent in order to match available mediation to the needs of the child and the prescribed SmartStart content.

Form 1: Profile of Mediator

Circle the average rating of functioning across the situations using the Mediated Learning Experience Rating Scale.

Mediator name: _____ Rater name: _____

Location: _____

Dates:

Prior to entry into the program _____

Post completion of the program _____

Type of Interaction	4 = Optimal	3 = Moderate	2 = Minimal	1 = Not Evident	NA = Not Applicable
Intentionality	4	3	2	1	NA
Meaning	4	3	2	1	NA
Bridging	4	3	2	1	NA
Joint Regard	4	3	2	1	NA
Sharing	4	3	2	1	NA
Task Regulation	4	3	2	1	NA
Praise and Encouragement	4	3	2	1	NA
Psychological Differentiation	4	3	2	1	NA
Challenge	4	3	2	1	NA
Contingent Responsiveness	4	3	2	1	NA
Affective Involvement	4	3	2	1	NA
Change	4	3	2	1	NA

To provide remediation for the needs of the mediator, it is best to share the actual profile with them and discuss each of the components as observed in their interactions. If the parents have completed their own Rating Scale as above, it would be useful to compare their perceptions of themselves with those of the consultant. In communicating with the parents, it is important to acknowledge what they are already doing well. Areas of need can be mutually determined, with shared ideas about how these are best addressed. Priorities need to be set, as it can be overwhelming to tackle too large a number simultaneously. We recommend special attention to Bridging, as this is often omitted from interactions by both teachers and parents, and is especially important to the development of abstract thought.

Determining the Needs of the Child

Just as it "takes two to tango," it certainly takes two to create a MLE. Mediation cannot be successful without the child's Reciprocity, which we call Responsiveness or Responsivity. On the one hand, the child's level and nature of responsiveness dictate the outcomes of the MLE; on the other hand, they significantly impact the mediator's ability to provide mediation. One of the challenging aspects of parenting an internationally adopted child is the child's ability to be a responsive partner. The consultant in this case needs to work with parents on their ability to read the child's cues, as well as with the child to be a better cue-sender to become available for mediation. The parents of international adoptees may have fabulous potential for mediation, but the process does not turn into a MLE unless there is reciprocity on the part of the child. Here is one example of such difficulty occurring when one of the authors (Lidz) taught a summer preschool class. A child entered the program who was truly feral. He had had virtually no socialization experiences, at least, none that were positive. During one interaction with his peers, another boy reached out to touch him. He interpreted this as an aggressive act and hit the child. The role of the mediator was to become an interpreter. It was necessary to let the new child know that the gesture was a positive attempt to become a friend and not an aggressive act. The child who reached out also needed to hear this interpretation so that further attempts to make friends would not be suppressed.

Research with the MLERS made it apparent that Reciprocity has its own characteristics that are best captured on a scale of its own. Based on interactions during the same activities involved in the interaction observations with the parents, the child's behaviors are rated on the RMS. The full Scale initially appeared in the Lidz (2003, pp. 124–126)

"Early Childhood Assessment" book. The components of the RMS are represented in a Profile in Table 2 below. This is completed by the mediator following the same interactional situations to which the MLERS applies, but this time it is the child's, not the mediator's, behaviors that are rated. First, the professional psychologist or social worker completes the full rating scale, and then transfers these scores onto the Profile. As with any of the scales, it is important to write descriptive comments to paint a picture of how these components look in action. This will be especially important when providing feedback to the parents. "Pre"/"Post" refers to program participation, that is, prior to entry into the program, and post completion of the program. As was the case for the MLERS, the ratings represent the average of the scores for each situation. Researchers who are interested in exploring the effects of the situation on the mediator and child can derive separated scores for each.

Form 2: Response to Mediation Profile

Circle the average rating of functioning across the situations using the *Response to Mediation Rating Scale.*

Child's name _____ Rater's name: _____
Location: _____

Dates:

Prior to entry into the program _____
Post completion of the program _____

Type of Interaction	4 = Optimal	3 = Moderate	2 = Minimal	1 = Not Evident	NA = Not Applicable
Self-regulation of attention	4	3	2	1	NA
Self-regulation of emotion	4	3	2	1	NA
Self-regulation of motor activity	4	3	2	1	NA
Evidence of strategic problem-solving	4	3	2	1	NA
Evidence of self-talk when working on a challenging task	4	3	2	1	NA
Turn-taking interactions with Mediator	4	3	2	1	NA
Responsiveness to Mediator Initiatives	4	3	2	1	NA
Comprehension of task	4	3	2	1	NA
Response to Challenge	4	3	2	1	NA
Interest in tasks and materials	4	3	2	1	NA

Finding or Making the Match in The SmartStart Toolbox Program

Please note that the full scales described here, along with information about their administration, interpretation, and research can be found in Lidz (1991, 2003). What is not included in these other publications is the information on The SmartStart Toolbox Program and its use as a remedial treasure chest of intervention ideas within the broader Dynamic Assessment model. The Scales described above allow the reader to turn SmartStart into a real tool. Of course, we could say that all the children need the whole set of tools regardless of the nature of their needs. However, we believe in efficiency and in the value of the

Table 4.1 SmartStart Toolbox Units and activities that address the child's mediation needs

	Area of Child Response	Applicable activities
1	Self-regulation of attention	Unit 1, Parts 1, 2 Unit 4, Part 1, Activity 1 Unit 6, Part 1, Activity 5
2	Self-regulation of emotion	Unit 3, Part 1, Activity 3 Unit 3, Part 2, Activity 3
3	Self-regulation of motor activity	Unit 1, Part 2, Activity 2 Unit 3, Part 1, Activity 1 Unit 6, Part 1, Activity 1
4	Evidence of Strategic problem-solving	Unit 2, Part 1, Activity 1
5	Evidence of self-talk when working on a challenging task	Unit 4, Part 2, Activity 3
6	Turn-taking interactions with Mediator	Unit 2, Part 1, Activity 2 Unit 4, Part 2, Activity 1 Unit 4, Part 3, Activity 5 Unit 6, Part 1, Activity 8
7	Responsiveness to mediator Initiatives	Unit 2, Part 1 Activity 3 Unit 5, Part 1, Activity 5 Unit 6, Part 1, Activity 2
8	Comprehension of task	Unit 3, Part 1 Unit 5, Part 1, Activity 1 Unit 5, Part 1, Activity 3
9	Response to Challenge	Unit 5, Part 2, Activity 3 Unit 5, Part 1, Activity 2
10	Interest in tasks and materials	Any of the activities that involve objects/toys

time and effort of both the professionals and the participating families and recommend the use of the activity chart below.

The final step of this model is to make the match between the child's needs for mediation and the appropriate activities in *The SmartStart Toolbox Program*. One important principle of this approach, as well as other mediation-based approaches to assessment and remediation, is to offer mediation only when it is needed. If the child has no need for mediation, then there is likely to be little reciprocity, and without reciprocity – no MLE. This model relies on explicit identification of the child's mediation needs, with prescriptive interventions from within the Program that directly target these needs. Determination of the parents' needs to optimize their mediational interactions are separated out, since their intervention is not offered within the parameters of *The SmartStart Toolbox Program*, but is assumed to be an aspect of the training of the consultants who work with the parents as clients. Identification of the area in need of improvement can sometimes provide sufficient intervention to change the behavior of the parents. That is, for some parents, it is sufficient to simply point to and discuss the MLE components with low ratings to make a difference in their interactions. For such parents, the addition of periodic review of video recordings can comprise an impactful teaching context.

In Table 3 we designate the unit and, if needed, the specific activities that address the child's needs identified in the Response to Mediation Profile. In some cases, the entire unit is suggested. In other cases, the needs are best addressed by specific activities. The recommendations in Table 3 are not exhaustive. All of the activities throughout the Program involve multiple goals and processes. They are assigned to one particular unit on the basis of primary focus. We have pulled some out for placement in Table 3 for the purpose of demonstration.

Child responsiveness characteristics such as Turn-Taking, Comprehension, Regulation of Emotion, and Attention are aspects of most activities, so almost anything you select can be appropriate, depending upon your focus. The mediator may instruct workshop participants to select a complex activity and repeat it with changing the focus. We recommend that the parents share with their child just what it is that they want him or her to get out of the activity. There is no reason to keep this a secret. For example, if a parent wants to help the child learn to improve control over motor movements, then just say that, with the additional comment of "Let's see if this helps. We'll talk about it afterward." The open sharing of intent will only help your child to internalize the goals and methods of the Program, and give them a feeling of having more control over their lives. The children themselves may come up with their own ideas of how to make extensions and elaborations.

We hope that the details of this model are sufficiently clear to enable professional consultants to attempt to use the Program in practice with clients. There are a few balls to juggle and, to use another metaphor, a few pieces to assemble in this puzzle. We hope you will find it sufficiently worth your while to make the attempt. This isn't a test, and no one will grade your success. You will see the effects one way or another in your clients, and modifications can and should be made in response to the feedback you receive from them. The usage of the Toolbox suggests the process of construction. Some scaffolds and mediations are offered here for your work. Classify this under the MLERS component of "joint regard." It is a tango for two, or three, or …

References

Feuerstein, R., Hoffman, M., Rand, Y. & Miller, R. (1980) *Instrumental enrichment*: Baltimore: University Park Press.

Lidz, C.S. (1991). *Practitioner's guide to dynamic assessment*. New York: Guilford.

Lidz, C.S. (2003). *Early childhood assessment*. Hoboken, NJ: Wiley.

Conclusion

How the SmartStart Toolbox Differs from Other Remedial Programs

We often hear the saying "it takes a village to raise a child" and nothing could be more relevant to bringing up an international adoptee. The coordinated efforts of the parents, school, professionals, and state-run agencies are needed to provide these children with the real opportunity to realize their potential. No less important are the methods of rehabilitation and remediation. These are the clinical procedures, teaching tools, and parenting techniques that are needed to scaffold the victims of prolonged neglect to graduate to the level of becoming self-sufficient and productive members of our society. The description of one such methodology, reflecting current research and best clinical practice, is the substance of this book.

What is the difference between The SmartStart Toolbox Program and other remedial programs for preschoolers and grades students in the early grades? This is the first and, at this point the only, remedial program developed specifically for use with internationally adopted children in this age group (pre-school and elementary school-age). The SmartStart Toolbox Program was designed on the basis of what is currently known about best practices in promoting the mental and social/emotional development of traumatized and neglected young children. Most other remedial programs for this age focus on milestones of child development, or on the content that children need to learn for early schooling, or on behavior management. These are, of course, relevant and important entities. But there are no publications to help teach adoptive parents and the professionals who work with them to provide scaffolds for children whose development was negatively affected by trauma, neglect, and deprivation while, at the same time, facilitating the development of the children's attachment to their new families. The program has two intertwined goals: to remediate cognitive and language domains of recently adopted foreign orphanage residents and to

DOI: 10.4324/9781003253587-6

facilitate the formation of attachment between adoptive parents and their adopted children via joint/shared activities. This is the mission of *The SmartStart Toolbox Program*: this is what allows a Start to be Smart, and this is what we hope will happen for our participants. Happy SmartStarting!

> "Shall We Dance?"
> © C.S. Lidz
> First the music,
> Then the moves,
> I'll start the steps.
> You're in the groove!
> Now take our turns
> As each one improves.
> It's no fun to dance alone.
> We need a pair
> To make a zone.

Index

Note: Page numbers in **bold** indicate tables; those in *italics* indicate figures.

abstract thought 25
"Adoption LifeBook" activity 89
Affective Warmth (Mediated Learning Experience) 102, 103
"All the World's a Stage" activity 83
alternative (That's Fantastic! vocabulary) **57**
anxiety 38–39
apprenticeship interaction 17
attachment 18–19, 20, 38; *see also* Making Connections to Strengthen Attachment
attention (Who Is in Charge? vocabulary) **84**
authoritative vs. authoritarian parents 78

"Because I Said so!" activity 66–67
Berchin-Weiss, J. 1
bilingualism 19
"Blotter Blobs" activity 54–55
body: "Mirror, Mirror!" activity 81; "Moving Experience" activity 32; "Red Light" activity 81–82; "Relax" activity 80–81
Bridging (Mediated Learning Experience) 100, 101, 103
"Brooklyn Bridge" game 87

cause (Making Connections to Strengthen Attachment vocabulary) **92**

"Cereal Serial" activity 31
Certificate of Completion *95*
Challenge (Mediated Learning Experience) 102, 103, 104
change: Making Connections to Strengthen Attachment vocabulary **92**; Mediated Learning Experience 99, 100, 101
"Change the Story" activity 56
characteristic (Noticing Our World vocabulary) **36**
Chase-Childers, L. 1
classifying by shape, color, size 16, 25, 33–35
"Cloud Nine" activity 52
clue (What's the Big Idea vocabulary) **75**
cognitive language, enrichment of 14, 16
cognitive skills: developmentally hierarchical nature of 15–16; formation and scaffolding of 14, 16; school readiness 10
"Collector" activity 33–34
compare (Noticing Our World vocabulary) **36**
comparing by shape, color, size 16, 25, 33–35
competence and motivation, relationship between 7
comprehension 108, **108**
concentration 39
confidence 39

content-oriented vs. process-oriented questions 39, 70
Contingent Responsiveness (Mediated Learning Experience) 101, 102, 103
cooperation 38
"Copycat" game 88
count (Nimble Symbol vocabulary) **67**
COVID-19 pandemic 6
create (That's Fantastic! vocabulary) **57**
creativity 50–56
cultural background 91–92
cultural internalization 14, 17
culture (Making Connections to Strengthen Attachment vocabulary) **92**

delayed gratification 79
describe (Noticing Our World vocabulary) **36**
"Details; Details ..." activity 27–28
Developmental Trauma Disorder 4–5
diagnostic-prescriptive process 96–108
different (Noticing Our World vocabulary) **36**
Donaldson Adoption Institute 8
Dynamic Assessment 97, 108

effect (Making Connections to Strengthen Attachment vocabulary) **92**
efficiency 70
emotion: and learning 87; "When You're Happy and You Know It ..." activity 83–84
emotional volatility 79
emotional vulnerability 10
Encouragement and Praise (Mediated Learning Experience) 101, 103, 104
environmental experience 25–30
evaluate (Let's Make a Plan vocabulary) **48**
executive functions 16, 77
explore 40–43; Let's Make a Plan vocabulary **48**
"Explore-a-toy" activity 42–43
extra-linguistic supports 20
"Eye Blinking Context" game 87

family (Making Connections to Strengthen Attachment vocabulary) **92**
"Family Fun" activity 64–65
family relationships 88–89, 90–92
fanciful thinking 52–55
fantasy 50–56
Feuerstein 14, 16, 17, 70, 78, 99
"Finding the Source" activity 90
"First Say; then Do" activity 82
food: "Cereal Serial" activity 31; "Details; Details ..." activity 27; "Kitchen Capers" activity 44–45; "Make 'em and Bake 'em" activity 54; "Object Hide and Seek" activity 41–42; "Sense-a-tional Food!" activity 29–30
future 38; Let's Make a Plan vocabulary **48**

generalization 69–70
gestures 61–62
"Getting to Know You" activity 45–46
"Giant Walk" game 87
Gindis, B. 1
goal (Let's Make a Plan vocabulary) **48**
goal setting: Let's Make a Plan 38, 44–47; That's Fantastic! 50
grapho-motor skills 15–16
gratification, delayed 79
group (Noticing Our World vocabulary) **36**
"Guess What is in the Mouth" game 87

"Headlines" activity 71–72
"Home Theatre" activity 46–47
hypothesis (That's Fantastic! vocabulary) **57**

"If I Were ..." activity 53–54
"if ... then" connections 16
imagination 50–56; That's Fantastic! vocabulary **57**
"Important New Day" activity 40–41
impulsivity 77, 79–80, 82
"I'm Puzzled" activity 44
"I'm thinking of ..." game 29–30

inferential thinking 55–56
Intentionality (Mediated Learning Experience) 99, 102, 103
interest in tasks and materials **108**
internalization of culture 14, 16
"I Spy" activity 34–35
"It's About Rhyme" activity 66
"It's the Principle of the Thing" activity 74–75
"I've Got to Get Organized" activity 43

Joint Regard (Mediated Learning Experience) 99–100, 102, 103, 108

"Kitchen Capers" activity 44–45

language: acquisition 8, 10–11, 19–20, 51; cognitive, enrichment of 14, 15; extra-linguistic supports 20; play 51; as psychological tool 17, 19–20; school readiness 10–11; and self-regulation 78
leaf collection activity 33–34, 98
learned helplessness 16
Let's Make a Plan 23, 38–49; exploring and organizing 40–43; goal setting, strategies, implementing and amending the plan 44–47; mediator response questions 49; objectives 40; theory 38–40; vocabulary list **48**
"Let's Play Together" activity 87–88
"Let's Think About It!" 1
letter (Nimble Symbol vocabulary) **67**
"Let Them Read History" activity 91–92
Lidz, C.S. 1, 97, 99, 103, 105; Did You Ever Notice? 25; Family 86; Imagination 50; It is nice to have a tool! v; "Let's Think About It" 1; Planning 38; Rules 69; Shall We Dance? 112; Symbols 59; Who's in charge? 77
Lifebooks 89
"Listen up!" activity 83
Luria, A. 78

main ideas 71–73
"Make 'em and Bake 'em" activity 54

Making Connections to Strengthen Attachment 23, 86–93; family relationships 90–92; mediator response questions 93; objectives 87; theory 86; vocabulary list **92**
matching Units to mediation needs 106–108, **107**
mathematics 59
Meaning (Mediated Learning Experience) 100, 103, 104
"Measure for Pleasure" activity 65
Mediated Learning Experience (MLE) 14, 16, 17, 96, 98–104, 106; Rating Scale (MLERS) 98–103, 104, 108
mediational approach 16
Mediator Profile 102–103
memory 16; connecting learning with emotion 87; "To See Is to Remember" activity 30
"Mirror, Mirror!" activity 81
monolingualism 19
motivation: and competence, relationship between 7; task-intrinsic, facilitation of 14, 16; That's Fantastic! 50, 51
"Moving Experience" activity 32
"My Secret Language" activity 61–62

nature walk 33–34, 98
Nimble Symbol 23, 59–68; creating symbols 61–63; mediator response questions 68; objectives 60; recognizing symbols 61; theory 59–60; using symbols 63–67; vocabulary list 67
"No", difficulty with 79
notice (Noticing Our World vocabulary) **36**
Noticing Our World 23, 25–37; comparing and classifying by shape, color, size 33–35; learning how to look, listen, touch, and be aware of the surroundings 25–30; mediator response questions 37; objectives 26; pattern recognition and production 31–33; theory 25–26; vocabulary list **36**
number (Nimble Symbol vocabulary) **67**

"Object Hide and Seek"
    activity 41–42
"older" children 4, 6, 7–9
O'Malley, B. 89
organizing 40–43
"Our Family Shield" activity 63

parties 46
past (Making Connections
    to Strengthen Attachment
    vocabulary) **92**
"Pasta Sort" activity 35
pattern (Noticing Our World
    vocabulary) **36**
"Pattern Pictures" activity 32–33
pattern recognition and production
    16, 25, 31–33
phonemic awareness 59
"Pillow ride" game 87
plan (Let's Make a Plan
    vocabulary) **48**
"Planned TV Watching (or, Who's
    in Control of This, Anyway?)"
    activity 47
planning 16; *see also* Let's
    Make a Plan
play: "Let's Play Together" activity
    87–88; "Play Time!" activity 52–53;
    "Rules of the Game" activity 74;
    That's Fantastic! **57**, 58
play dates 45–46
"Play Time!" activity 52–53
Praise and Encouragement (Mediated
    Learning Experience) 101, 103, 104
precise (What's the Big Idea
    vocabulary) **75**
predict (That's Fantastic!
    vocabulary) **57**
predictions 55–56
prepare (Let's Make a Plan
    vocabulary) **48**
present (Making Connections
    to Strengthen Attachment
    vocabulary) **92**
principle 69, 74–75; What's the Big
    Idea vocabulary **75**
process-oriented vs. content-oriented
    questions 39, 70
professionals: diagnostic-prescriptive
    process 96–109; tips for 20

Profiles: Mediator 102–103; Response
    to Mediation 104–105
Psychological Differentiation
    (Mediated Learning Experience)
    101, 103
psychological tools 14, 16, 20;
    language 16, 19–20
psychologists *see* professionals

read (Nimble Symbol vocabulary) **67**
reading: Nimble Symbol 59, 63–64;
    "You Tell Me Yours and I'll Tell
    You Mine" activity 71
"Ready, Set, Read" activity 63–64
real (That's Fantastic! vocabulary) **57**
reality and fantasy, distinguishing
    between 51
"Red Light" activity 81–82
relationship (Making Connections
    to Strengthen Attachment
    vocabulary) **92**
"Relax" activity 80–81
remediation 4–7; connecting learning
    to emotion 14; conventional
    15; difference between The
    SmartStart Toolbox Program and
    other programs 110–111; school
    readiness 11–12
"Remember Me" game 88
represent (Nimble Symbol
    vocabulary) **67**
response to challenge **108**
Response to Mediation Profile
    104–105, 106
Response to Mediation Scale (RMS)
    99, 104
responsiveness of child 103–104;
    matching Units and activities to
    mediation needs **107**
rhyme 66
"Ritually Speaking" activity 90–91
rules 69, 70, 73–74; self-regulation 79;
    What's the Big Idea? vocabulary **75**
"Rules for My Space" activity 73–74
"Rules of the Game" activity 74

school readiness 4, 9–13
self-control: Who Is in Charge?
    vocabulary **84**; *see also* Who Is in
    Charge?

self-regulation 23, 77–85; of attention 108, **108**; of emotion 108, **108**; encouragement of 14, 17; Let's Make a Plan 38; matching Units and activities to mediation needs 108, **108**; of motor activity **108**; school readiness 11; That's Fantastic! 50; Who Is in Charge? vocabulary **84**; *see also* Who Is in Charge?

self-talk **108**

"Sense-a-tional Food!" activity 29–30

senses 25–30

sequencing 15; "Cereal Serial" activity 31; Noticing Our World vocabulary **36**

Sharing (Mediated Learning Experience) 101, 103, 104

"Signs of the Times" activity 61

similar (Noticing Our World vocabulary) **36**

"Simon Says" game 66, 67

"smell and tell" game 30

social context of learning 14, 16

social skills: reciprocal interaction 16; school readiness 10

social workers *see* professionals

special needs children 4, 6, 12

strategic problem-solving **108**

strategic thinking 38, 39, 44–47

strategy (Let's Make a Plan vocabulary) **48**

symbols: Nimble Symbol vocabulary **67**; use of 16; *see also* Nimble Symbol

"Symbols in My Home" activity 62

"Taking Turns as Boss" activity 84

task-intrinsic motivation, facilitation of 14, 15

Task Regulation (Mediated Learning Experience) 100, 102, 103

"taste and tell" game 30

television *see* TV

"tell me which one" game 28

That's Fantastic! 23, 50–58; fanciful thinking 52–55; making inferences and predictions 55–56; mediator response questions 58; objectives 51; theory 50–51; vocabulary list **57**

theoretical background 14–21

think (That's Fantastic! vocabulary) **57**

thumb wrestling 88

"To See Is to Remember" activity 30

turn-taking 108, **108**

TV: "Planned TV Watching (or, Who's in Control of This, Anyway?)" activity 47; "TV Gab" activity 72–83

Vygotsky, L.S. 14, 17, 78

"We're Connected" activity 88–89

"What if ...?" activity 55–56

"What Is This?" activity 27

What's the Big Idea? 23, 69–76; main ideas 71–73; mediator response questions 76; objectives 71; principles and rules 73–75; theory 69–70; vocabulary list **75**

"When You're Happy and You Know It ..." activity 83–84

Who Is in Charge? 23, 77–85; main ideas 80–84; mediator response questions 85; objectives 80; theory 77–80; vocabulary list **84**

workshop program evaluation 93–94

write (Nimble Symbol vocabulary) **67**

"You Tell Me Yours and I'll Tell You Mine" activity 71

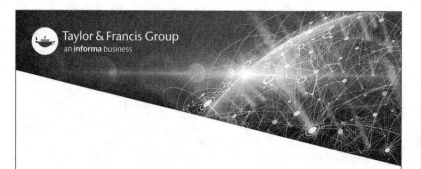

Printed in the United States
by Baker & Taylor Publisher Services